P9-BAW-930

MASK AND SCENE

MASK
AND
SCENE

An introduction to
a world view of theatre

Diana Devlin

90-985

The Scarecrow Press, Inc.
Metuchen, N.J.
1989

British edition published in 1989 by Higher and Further
Education Division, Macmillan Publishers Ltd.

British Library Cataloguing-in-Publication data available

Library of Congress Cataloging-in-Publication Data

Devlin, Diana.
  Mask and scene : an introduction to a world view of
theatre / Diana Devlin.
    p. cm.
  Bibliography: p.
  Includes index.
  ISBN 0-8108-2234-2 (alk. paper)
  1. Theater.   I. Title.
PN2021.D49   1989   89-33471
792—dc20

Contents

1

Worldwide theatre

In 1986, the English director Peter Brook mounted a production in Paris of *The Mahabharata*, an Indian story cycle, using an acting company drawn from England, Germany, Poland, India, Italy, Upper Volta, the United States, France, Japan, Lebanon and Gabon. During the same period a Japanese film *Ran*, directed by Akira Kurosawa, was released worldwide; it was based on plays by Shakespeare, especially *King Lear*. These two examples show that, like sport, theatre has become an international activity.

Until the twentieth century, most countries developed local, regional and national traditions of theatre. Theatre history books are therefore usually divided into chapters describing developments at various times in different countries, such as Ancient Greece and the Italian Renaissance. But today it is more useful to consider together aspects of theatre from different historical and geographic areas. Instead of dividing chapters according to history and geography, this book examines different elements in the art of theatre.

Theatre conventions

The art of theatre involves people speaking and moving, often very much as they do in ordinary life. For that reason it is not easy to define exactly which activities are theatre and which are not. In the playground, street or garden, we see children playing pretend games, sometimes dressing up to add to the fun. We may have noticed adults changing their behaviour to suit different situations (a teacher behaving differently when a more senior teacher is present, or a parent who looks and acts differently at home and at work). They are adopting roles to suit the various situations in life in which they find themselves. Sometimes whole groups dress up and behave in a special way, at a wedding, for example, or in a court of law. Many social occasions and community activities are prepared and rehearsed like a theatrical production. This book helps you to define theatre by examining the conventions, the rules of the game, which have been used at various times and places. Each chapter considers the conventions used for one element of production. To get a clear picture of the whole art, you need to read the book right through.

What is meant by theatre

In general terms theatre is, on the one hand, a group of people getting together to perform a play; on the other hand, a group of people getting together to see it. The word *theatre* was originally used to describe a place, but it can be used to describe everything that goes on there as well. The word *play* comes from the verb 'to play' and means what is done in a theatre. Often people use it in a more limited sense to mean the written text of what is played. You can also use the words *drama* (which means the action that is done on the stage), *performance* or *production*. All these words are used in other areas of life too. For example:

> *theatre* of war, operating *theatre*
> to *play* the piano, to *play* football
> human *drama*
> *performance* of a car, *performance* of a duty
> food *production*, mass *production*

Sometimes words are used in ordinary life to suggest that something is like theatre (and this is not always said as a compliment). What do you think is meant when something is described as 'theatrical' or 'dramatic'? Or when they say 'It's all such a performance, such a production'? There are many other words used in the theatre and also outside it, both with a theatrical and a non-theatrical meaning. The two words in the title, *mask* and *scene*, are other examples. You can wear a gas-mask, you can 'mask' your true feelings. Some actors have worn masks. The image of a mask, especially those of comedy and tragedy, is often used to symbolise the art of acting. *Scene* has a double meaning even in the theatre. It can mean a self-contained section of the drama, or the background and surroundings to the action on stage. We use both these meanings in life, too. ('Please don't make a scene about it,' or 'She turned the corner and saw a lovely scene'.

This two-way process gives an indication of the closeness of theatre to ordinary life. Compared with the other arts, theatre is more like life as we experience it day by day. It shows us real people in a real place for the duration of real time. Yet, throughout the history of theatre, audiences have been able to distinguish play, drama or theatre from the everyday world without difficulty. They have learnt, with some interesting exceptions, to believe in the onstage events, and yet not to believe them; to take part but not actively. This is because they have accepted a set of conventions which establish the boundaries between what is everyday life and what is theatre.

People made this distinction between theatre and life long before they looked for a word to describe what they were doing. For example, archaic tribes, both now and in the past, have performed ritual drama as part of the socio-religious life of their community. Historians sometimes call such activities the *origins* of theatre, as if they were not really to be counted as theatre. But theatrical activity takes place in many areas of life besides the professional, amateur and educational theatre worlds; for example, in children's play, therapy and wider forms of training. In many civilised communities, traditions of primitive folk drama survive to enrich the culture. Again, some people would draw a distinction between such activities and real theatre. However, in this book, they are considered as belonging to the art of theatre.

Theatre and the human story

The story of world theatre, if it could be told, is at least ten thousand years old. Human beings have existed, in more or less the same biological form we are now, for longer than that. For at least that long, since the end of the Ice Age, they have formed communities and performed plays. We know this from scattered evidence of rituals, found in different parts of the world. The study of such evidence is usually the field of archaeology and anthropology, not theatre history.

Therefore, even the evidence that exists is rarely presented in a way that allows us to analyse its theatrical form. But whenever an account of archaic ritual implies the taking on of roles, or the acting-out of a situation, we know we are in the field of theatre.

Human beings first evolved in the continent of Africa. They spread outwards from there to the rest of Africa, to Europe, Asia and Indonesia, then further afield to the Americas and Australasia. Twenty thousand years ago they had settled in all these parts and were developing community rituals to act out beliefs about their existence. Whichever area of the world interests you, you may read the available evidence on these early forms of theatre, and analyse them into the same constituent parts as any other kind of theatre.

When the Ice Age ended, Australasia and the Americas were isolated. Until the colonisation of the New World in the sixteenth century, their cultures developed separately from those in the great landmass of Europe, Africa and Asia. In each of these cultures, ceremonial and spontaneous theatre must have played some part, but except where archaeological evidence survives, we have no proof of it. Other evidence of early theatre comes from surviving archaic groups, such as American Indians, African tribes and Australian aborigines. Hunting, agriculture and ancestor worship formed the basis of much ritual drama.

The first civilisations sprang up in Mesopotamia and Egypt. The word *civilisation* comes from the word for city. It implies a more complex, more sophisticated culture, not necessarily a superior culture. More civilisations sprang up in a broad belt of lands that spread out from the equator. They are marked by the development of social and religious structures.

In Africa, the Sahara desert isolated such civilisations as Ghana, Mali and Songhai. In Central and South America, the civilisations of the Incas, the Mayans and the Aztecs flourished and declined without contact from outside. In Europe and Asia, various civilisations grew, flourished, spread and declined, or were wiped out, especially when North European tribes came south and vandalised their cultures. In many of these cultures little direct evidence of theatre has come down to us, but in some of them, such as Greece, Rome, India, China, Japan and Indonesia, theatre began to be recognised as a definable form of activity. This means that the official history of theatre often begins with these cultures, following the progression of theatre, mainly chronologically, from about 500 BCE. (The Christian counting of years is so universal that it is best to use it for all cultures, but to refer to the years as CE, for Common Era, or BCE, for Before Common Era.) However, the beginning of *official* theatre in any civilisation does not eradicate the archaic forms. Theatre is like dress fashion. Fashions change, but people away from the big cities continue to wear whatever they find pleasing and practical, hardly changing over hundreds of years. So it is with theatre. It continued in all kinds of forms, sometimes merging with the established theatre, sometimes developing into other areas of life, such as games and sports. In civilisations in which we know theatrical activity was disapproved of, there are records showing that it survived nevertheless. For example, during the early centuries of Christianity, the Roman Catholic Church condemned plays and acting, but they kept on issuing edicts to forbid it, so people must have kept on doing it. These records of condemnation are evidence for the continuity of popular theatre, that is, theatre of the common people.

The theatre of early and intermediate cultures was closely connected with priesthood and kingship. Cultures developed around organised religions which defined and controlled both secular and spiritual lives of their followers. Drama was inextricably linked with ceremony and myth. It was valued according to a prescribed ethical code. These religions split Europe and Asia into separate cultures, largely isolated from each other. There was Christendom in the West, which split into the territory that followed Roman Catholicism, and the territory that was Orthodox. In the East, there were several religions, each dominating the culture in which they were followed: Judaism, Hinduism, Buddhism, Taoism, Confucianism and later Islam. The cultural split between East and West continued for several hundred years, but once it was bridged, it became clear that theatre had developed in various parallel ways, which offer interesting and illuminating comparisons. The conventions that we find in European theatre up to 1500 are different, but not radically different, from conventions in various forms of Eastern theatre.

However, around the time of the sixteenth century, a cultural corner was turned in Europe. In and around Shakespeare's time, religion, science and the arts were revolutionised, the New World was discovered and colonialism began. There began the centuries of rapid development which brought the West to the dominant position it held by the nineteenth century. During these centuries the established theatre in the West developed along such firm lines that it seemed it must be the best and only kind of theatre there could be. European styles of theatre were exported to America and spread to Russia. But the Eastern theatre continued to develop along its own lines. Many of the examples in this book will point to the contrast between the theatrical styles in the West and in the East.

In the twentieth century the different worlds have begun to be joined in terms of theatre, as in other things. Western and Eastern traditions have borrowed from each other. The power of archaic theatre has begun to be valued, both in its surviving forms and from accounts of early communities. Popular forms of theatre have also been drawn upon. Immigrant and native traditions are just beginning to feed into each other. All this leads to a *whole world* theatre. Not a homogeneous kind of theatre the same the whole world over – though some elements of theatre are international and multicultural – but a theatre in which each performance draws on whichever traditions express that community's needs and beliefs the best.

A personal angle

Whatever subject you study, you bring your own knowledge and experience to it. This personal angle is particularly important to theatre, because it is based on what is *here* and *now*. Yet it also provides the opportunity for us to experience, at second-hand, the lives of other people, either within our own society, or somewhere else. This book attempts to set you on the path of recognising or searching out beliefs and theatrical traditions in the part of the world you are in now and in other parts.

You will find that many of the examples in the book are taken from Shakespeare. This is for several reasons. The plays of William Shakespeare were written at a pivotal time in the cultural history of the world. His age therefore provides an interesting vantage point from which to view a vast range of theatrical activity. Another reason is that the works of Shakespeare are studied, performed and appreciated throughout the world. He is truly an international playwright. A third reason is that Shakespeare himself explored and commented on the art of theatre very fully. His own reflections often enlighten our understanding of theatre. Lastly, my own personal angle provides a reason, performances of Shakespeare having been the foundation of my theatrical experience.

Starting out from our own experience, we can extend it, so as to understand other people's, and gradually gain a perception of our place in the whole world. That is why we should try to take a world view of theatre as well as a personal view. Such an approach also shows us the vast range of opportunities that exist to create and study theatre. World travel and the information media have put within our grasp a far greater historical and geographical spread of theatrical resources than any society knew before. It is foolish not to draw upon them to enrich our own community's culture.

2

The theatre event

IT is 8.00 p.m. on Broadway, the theatre district of New York, New York, USA. You have purchased a ticket for a popular musical, selecting from over one hundred plays which are on that night. You enter the theatre, going through a spacious foyer to the auditorium, guided to a numbered seat. You sit facing the stage, like the other two thousand or so in the audience, watching and listening in silence, except when you laugh, applaud or talk during the interval. At the end of a couple of hours you leave, perhaps planning another visit to the theatre the next day, week, month or year. That is the pattern of theatre-going today in New York, London, Paris, Moscow, Tokyo, Sydney and many other cities of the world.

But there are other ways of experiencing theatre. In China, a visit to the Peking Opera might be over many hours, during which time you sit at a tea table with your friends, while several plays are presented, eating, drinking, cracking nuts, talking, going in and out when you feel like it, waving to people the other side of the theatre and generally behaving more casually than if you were at a cricket match.

Or imagine you are in a village in Poland on Christmas Eve sitting quietly at home with your family. Suddenly you hear voices. A group of rowdy schoolboys is outside. They burst into the house, dressed in garish costumes and proceed to act out the story of King Herod, weaving into it incidents from Polish history, or recent occurrences in the village. They swap parts, take suggestions from the audience and generally create a raucous, but highly enjoyable entertainment. At the end, they disappear, moving on swiftly to the next house.

These different patterns of behaviour have formed around the various ways of understanding what kind of occasion

theatre-going is, and how it is organised. It may be part of a
seasonal festival, a social celebration, or simply an opportunity
for a good time out. In this chapter we examine some of the
different kinds of theatre events.

Festivals and celebrations

A festival is a periodic celebration in which a whole
community is involved. Every culture marks important
occasions with a festival; many of these festivals include
theatre events.

Some of the oldest festivals were supplications or
thanksgivings for the most basic needs of life, such as food.
Evidence survives of very early rituals performed in connection
with hunting. Then, when humans discovered agriculture,
their rituals often centred on the cycle of the seasons, many
important festivals coinciding with the New Year. As early as
3000 BCE, a well-organised New Year Festival occurred at
Sumer (in present day Iraq), while in Ghana, people still
travel to the annual 'Hunger Hooting Festival' which
celebrates a victory over famine by the Ga people. These two
activities, hunting and agriculture, show us two different
kinds of timing for festivals. Hunting, and the rituals
associated with it, take place at variable times, when the
conditions are right; while agriculture is closely bound up
with the cycle of the seasons. Still today, some festivals (such
as weddings) occur at variable times, and others are annual
events, fixed by the calendar; for example, Christmas,
Hanukah, Chinese New Year, Ramadan, May Day.

While many festivals are linked to the seasonal cycle of the
year, others mark the stages in human life, while yet others
commemorate the history of a community, whether it is a
village, a city or a nation. The most important celebrations
connected with the span of human life are birth, initiation
into adulthood, and death. They are known as *rites of passage.*
Evidence survives of many dramatic celebrations of these
rites. For example, in Ancient Egypt, a ritual known as the
Abydos Passion Play was performed from about 2500 to
550 BCE, enacting the death rites of the mythical figure of
Osiris; while in many surviving tribal communities in
America, Australasia and Africa, important rituals are

enacted to mark the adolescents' initiation into adulthood, often with the sexes segregated.

The history of theatre is closely connected with the history of religion and politics. For many centuries after the rise of the first city-state at Sumer, the great world religions largely controlled both the politics and the theatre of the civilised world. The most elaborate theatre events were religious festivals authorised by the church, the temple or the elders of the community. In India, theatre flourished for several centuries in the Hindu temples. Temple dancers in India and Indonesia still make an important contribution to the performing arts. In Ancient Greece, dramatic festivals and competitions were major events. The most famous was the City Dionysos in Athens, founded in 534 BCE and performed as an annual spring festival in honour of the god Dionysos. It was organised as part of the community life of this city-state in which democracy was first practised. Some of the drama performed there still survives, in the plays of Aeschylus, Sophocles, Euripides and Aristophanes. This rich theatrical tradition strongly influenced the development of theatre in the Roman Empire, spreading throughout Europe.

In Europe and Asia, the early religious festivals of drama declined as the civilisations which produced them vanished, some of them destroyed by the descent of nomadic tribes from the north, such as Goths, Huns and Mongols, about fifteen hundred years ago. Only in China did arts and culture survive, including a dramatic tradition which developed in isolation from the rest of the world. Meanwhile other civilisations were developing, such as the Mayan, Aztec and Inca cultures in Central America and Peru, all with their dramatic rituals, such as the Mayan Dance of the Giants performed in celebration of the summer solstice. African civilisations also developed their own festivals. Numerous tribal ceremonies continued to thrive there and in America, while in Australia, the aboriginal tribes performed cycles of initiation ceremonies re-enacting the creative *dream time* of their ancestors.

In some religions, drama was not encouraged. The Christian Church began by rejecting the idea of theatre, but later embraced it. This dual attitude has continued throughout the history of Christianity. Islam rejected drama too, and its growth and influence contributed to the decline of theatre in many parts of the Islamic world. Yet one Islamic drama festival existed and survived until quite recently. The *ta'ziya*, known as the Persian Passion Play, was performed in the first ten days of the Moslem month of Muburran, by the Shiite Moslems, to commemorate the extermination of the Prophet's descendants. (Unlike orthodox Moslems, the Shiites believe that the Prophet's authority is carried through his descendants, not through appointed caliphs.) A passion play has also survived in Afghanistan.

The Feast of Corpus Christi

As an example of a theatre festival, let us take the Christian feast of Corpus Christi, around which a dramatic festival flourished in England and in other parts of Europe from about 1300 to 1500 CE. It was a festival in which artistic, intellectual and socio-economic life were inextricably linked with religion. It is difficult for us to imagine how much the story of Christ and its meaning affected the lives of ordinary people in the Middle Ages. We can get some idea by looking at the great Gothic cathedrals which still dominate many European cities, each built over several centuries, by hundreds of individual craftsmen. Each contains a mass of detail, from the intricate carving of the wooden *misericords* (the half-seats where monks could rest during long services) to the roof bosses, set high in the vaulted ceiling, almost too high to see, and the jewel-like mosaic of the stained-glass windows. However bizarre the individual carving, each detail forms part of an elaborate symmetry, expressing the strength and conviction of Christian belief.

Another example of the centrality of Christianity is the measurement and division of time. Hours of the day could often be distinguished by the sound of the church bell, announcing the regular services; the days, though named after pagan gods, stretched from Sunday, the holy day, through the weeks, with many other holy days (or 'holidays') celebrated in between. The Christian year was, and still is, divided to allow worship to emphasise different parts of the story of Christ, often paralleling the passing of the seasons and the pagan celebrations begun in an earlier era. Thus the dark days of Advent, foretelling the coming of Christ, who would bring light, culminate in the feast of Christmas, coinciding with the pagan Yuletide of the winter solstice. Later in the winter, the season of Lent, marked by a period of fasting, celebrates Christ's forty days spent wrestling with Satan in the wilderness. The Lenten fast is preceded by days of revelry and feasting called *Carnival*, which means 'putting aside meat'. This has continued as a festive period in many parts of the Christian and partly Christian world, such as the Caribbean. As spring approaches, the season when new life bursts through in nature, the passion, crucifixion and resurrection of Christ are celebrated, coinciding with the pagan festival of dawn, which was also celebrated at Eastertide. The weeks after Easter lead up to Whitsun, which celebrates the spread of Christ's message, and then Trinity, celebrating the unity of God as Father, Son and Holy Ghost. And so on, until Advent begins again. As social life demanded more divisions of time, they were still named by Christian days and season. The religious and social aspects of Catholic Christianity were indistinguishable when it was the unifying culture of Western Europe.

It was in this unified culture that the Corpus Christi plays developed and flourished. The feast of Corpus Christi, meaning 'the body of Christ', is on the Thursday after Trinity Sunday, which can be any time between 23 May and 24 June. It was established in 1311 to celebrate the central meaning of the Mass, the Christian service of Holy Communion. In the Mass, the priest imitates the words and actions of Christ at the Last Supper, when he broke bread with his disciples and said 'Take, eat, this is my body', and gave them wine saying 'Drink ye all of it; for this is my blood of the new testament, which is shed for many for the remission of sins' (Matthew 26–28).

The Catholic Church taught that every time the priest enacted this drama of the giving of bread and wine, a miracle occurred, transubstantiating the bread and wine into the body and blood of Christ. The Feast of Corpus Christi was established to celebrate this miracle which linked the life and death of Christ with every single Christian, whenever he or she attended the Mass. Thus, the root of the Corpus Christi plays lay in religious expression. However, the organisation and performance was carried out, not by the Church, but by the townspeople. It was fitting that such a miracle be celebrated through the people enacting for themselves the drama of Christ coming into the world to save them. At first the Feast was built around a procession, carrying the Blessed Sacrament around the town. Soon it developed into a full-blown dramatic festival.

Like the Gothic cathedrals, the plays of Corpus Christi were made up of many parts. They consisted of a cycle of up to forty-eight plays, combined to make a unified whole. Of those performed in England, four scripts survive, including those from York, Chester and Wakefield, and there is evidence that cycles were also performed at Ipswich, Kendal, Lincoln, Newcastle-on-Tyne, Norwich, Beverley, Worcester and other places.

Each cycle consisted of episodes from the Old and New Testaments. These were not haphazardly selected, but formed together the framework of belief on which the Christian faith was built. Beginning with the Creation, the cycles then depicted the Fall of Lucifer and the Fall of Man, showing how humanity thus stood in need of salvation. Episodes about the Nativity, the Crucifixion and the Resurrection of Christ followed, and in between came plays which prefigured Christ's coming, such as the story of Noah, who was saved from destruction. Last came episodes depicting the effect of Christ on humanity, such as the Harrowing of Hell, which showed the liberation of souls from Hell, and the Day of Judgement, when souls saved by Christ were finally judged by their deeds.

The Corpus Christi cycle was elaborately mounted, and performed at one or more locations in the town, either spread over several days (as at Chester) or lasting from dawn to dusk (as at York). The performances must have attracted the population of the town, and visitors from rural communities from miles around. Each episode was the responsibility of a craft guild, that is a group following one of the trades in the town. Another word for a special craft was *mystery*, which could also be used about special or secret religious acts. The cycles are therefore sometimes called mystery plays with something of a double meaning attached to the word. Often the episode traditionally undertaken by a guild was particularly appropriate to its work. For example, Noah's Flood was played by the Waterleaders and Drawers in the Dee at Chester, and by the Fishers and Mariners at York. At York, too, there was black humour in the fact that the Crucifixion play was undertaken by the Pynners, who made nails and pins.

While each play was short and simple, with a small cast, the scale of each whole cycle was enormous. The co-ordination of the entire presentation was as complicated as organising a Royal Wedding. The Town Council or Corporation undertook the organisation, while the scripts were probably written and compiled by members of the Church. In later years, there are records of actors being paid to perform in the plays, but rarely any instance of the audience paying to watch. By and large this was community drama, not professional entertainment. The Corpus Christi festival was the finest achievement of amateur drama, produced and acted as religious and civic celebration.

The first records of Corpus Christi cycles date from the 1370s. They flourished well into the 1500s, but then the Roman Catholic Church was split as the Protestant churches broke away from it. There was much social unrest, civil wars and religious persecutions. Protestants rejected the dogma of transubstantiation on which the true meaning of Corpus Christi rested. Religion as a topic of drama was gradually suppressed in England during the reign of Queen Elizabeth I and the performance of mystery cycles faded out, though Shakespeare may have had the chance to see them. They lasted longest in Catholic Spain, where *autos sacramentales* were finally prohibited in 1765.

Theatre occasions

Most major theatre festivals were annual occasions lasting many hours or several days. Anticipation, preparation, enjoyment and reflection all fitted into the cycle of the year, as Christmas or a summer holiday does now in Britain and other places. These great religious/civic occasions were largely amateur events. Prizes might be given, as they were at the City Dionysos in ancient Athens, and payments made, but many of the people involved had other occupations to return to.

Many other kinds of theatre have been non-professional, or semi-professional, and occasional. Apart from major seasonal festivals, there have always been other feasts, in town and country, worth celebrating with dancing, singing, revelry and plays. Other occasions have also been celebrated. Royal events, academic achievements, military victories, and other civic occasions, have throughout history been marked with pageants, processions, puppet shows, declamations, tableaux and dramatic contests.

All the drama we have mentioned so far had, or has, considerable significance for its audience. The great religious/civic dramas were important events, taking priority over all other activities, while they lasted. Folk drama and tribal rituals have often arisen out of the urgent need for a rich harvest, in order to gather strength to hunt, to conquer a neighbouring tribe, to mark the transition into adulthood, or to honour the dead. Often one of the purposes of the event was to teach people the established values and traditions of their society.

Interludes and entertainments

Theatre is also to be seen as an escape from the normal responsibilities of life, time away from the main activities, when troubles can be forgotten in the enjoyment of a fiction. Whether it is an interlude at a feast, performed between the courses, or a situation comedy on television, to be watched before doing the washing-up, or a night out on the town, theatre often invites its audience to leave aside work, conscience and responsibility.

This is where the world of entertainment begins. From the class clown, to the highly paid Hollywood star, those with comic or tragic skill have turned it on for the amusement of whatever audience they can find. Professional or amateur theatre for entertainment has probably been around for as long as human culture. Even in times and places where theatre is officially disapproved of, such as the Islamic world, it has evidently occurred, but no coherent account can exist of the casual entertainment that crops up in every community.

However, by comparing scattered accounts, visual evidence and surviving scripts or films, we can find some common features of popular entertainment, such as topical humour and satire, exaggeration, glamour and titillation, violence and sentiment.

These aspects of theatrical entertainment have much to do with the moral values of a society. There have been sections of society, and periods of history, when the moral balance has tipped towards decadence and permissiveness. The most notorious example was the last days of the Roman Empire, when spectacles of violence and depravity were accepted forms of entertainment. At other times, the balance has tipped the other way: authorities have imposed rigorous censorship upon the theatre, repressing free expression when it was considered to have a corrupting influence, either morally or politically; for example, under totalitarian governments such as Soviet Russia.

Theatre and learning

One area of life closely connected with drama is education. Every mother sees her child learning through playing, through make-believe and imitation. Theatre has often been used as a way of teaching a specific lesson. Examples are:

> a tribe in Tanzania, where the women perform two participatory dramas called *digubi*, to teach girls how to deal first with menstruation, and then with the sexual side of marriage;
> the medieval play of *Everyman*, which teaches Christian repentance;
> *Agitprop* drama, a term coined in the early twentieth century to describe European plays (especially Russian and German), devised for socio-political agitation and propaganda;
> village drama in India and other developing countries, devised to raise consciousness and teach self-sufficiency.

At various times throughout history, groups with a particular message to teach, or a sermon to preach, have used theatre as an immediate, effective and entertaining means of direct communication. This has never been more marked than in the last two decades, when feminism, racism, poverty and war have motivated the creation of radical theatre movements. In Britain particularly, the development of theatre for education has begun to play a distinct part in the total picture of theatre.

Theatre is also taught as a discipline in its own right. In many forms of Eastern theatre, training of the performers has traditionally been long and arduous, requiring total dedication. Such harsh regimes may seem somewhat inhuman to people in the West, yet the same kind of single-minded, rigorous training is required for sports, music and dance.

In general education, knowledge and appreciation of theatre is increasingly recognised as a worthwhile subject of study. In the West, this is often represented by a shift, in schools and colleges, from the academic study of dramatic literature to more practical courses. In the East and in the developing countries, it is seen in the growing appreciation and cultivation of traditional forms, which had begun to be lost under the strong influence of Western culture.

Thus there are three ways in which theatre and education have been linked:

The use of theatre as a teaching method, either through participation or observation.
Training for the theatre.
Knowledge and appreciation of theatre.

The last two aspects of education lead us on to another kind of theatre event.

Theatre as an artistic event

Not all communities recognise theatre as an art form, to be appreciated simply for its own sake. Often it is too closely connected with the other needs of the community to be separated. But in many societies, there has come a time of prosperity and peace, when either a privileged section, or the whole community, has enough leisure, confidence and pride to cultivate and appreciate, with conscious pleasure, the products of their own civilisation. That is when the arts of music, literature, theatre, painting and sculpture can be practised and enjoyed purely for themselves. Not surprisingly, this practice has usually originated in the wealthier, leisured classes, especially around royal or imperial courts. In Japan, for example, after 1400, the country cut itself off from outside influence and began a four-century period of virtual isolation. Theatre centres then developed in Tokyo and Kyoto. In Europe, after the flowering of theatre in Athens and Rome, one of the first great theatre centres to emerge was the Medici court in Florence, also during the fifteenth century. During this period, there was a rebirth of classical learning and the arts in Western Europe. Hence, the period is called the Renaissance. Much interchange of ideas and cultures occurred between the various European courts and seats of learning, many monarchs and nobility vying with each other to be the greatest patron of the arts. In this climate, the art of theatre thrived, drawing into itself the skills of music, painting and poetry, as well as acting. Italy, Spain, France and England led the way. Although European theatre had been dominated by the Church, it developed so independently during the sixteenth century that even the cataclysmic split between Roman Catholicism and Protestantism did not hinder it. Theatre continued to develop, as a powerful means of expression which appealed to the educated and to the unlearned, reaching its zenith in the theatre of Shakespeare's time.

It was in this period that the organisation and presentation of theatre began to be a continuous business operation, rather than a series of special occasions. As an example of this operation, let us take the theatre of Shakespeare's time.

The business of theatre in Shakespeare's time

Professional theatre begins when there is sufficient demand for someone to spend their working hours doing it and earning a living. When material conditions are hard, there is only time to watch theatre occasionally, if at all, so it is usually home-grown entertainment. When conditions are easier, there is more demand, but still not enough to keep entertainers occupied in one place. So actors have often been itinerant workers, travelling from place to place, earning their keep as they go. In North America, a novel style of travelling developed in the nineteenth century, in the form of showboats which paddled up and down the great rivers, stopping off en route to perform their plays, then moving on. Strolling players kept Europe entertained for hundreds of years, seeking out seasonal fairs and festivals where they knew people would gather in numbers. Surviving the winter is difficult for any travelling players who perform outside. In Northern Europe, the aim was to find a noble household to attach yourself to. Christmastide was a good time for plays and entertainments. Then, after the rigours of Lent and the joy of Eastertide, they would set out on the road again.

Between 1500 and 1600, the profession of theatre developed swiftly in Italy, Spain, France, England and other European countries. Theatre companies were established, theatres to house them were constructed, or suitable buildings converted. Royalty and noblemen sponsored lavish theatrical events, and large sections of the population enjoyed a colourful variety of plays. In England, this was the age of Shakespeare, one of the most flourishing eras of theatrical activity ever known. Shakespeare's own company of players was in the forefront of these times, and helped to establish theatre as a glorious art.

The sixteenth century was a time of great turmoil in England, especially in religion and politics. When Queen Elizabeth I came to the throne in 1558, there was much to be done to bring peace and stability to the country. Many laws were brought in, to mend the splits which the Reformation (the break-up of the Catholic Church) had torn, and to build a cohesive society. Actors, who did not seem to belong anywhere, were in danger of being classed with rogues and vagabonds, and punished for being vagrants, if they could not give the name of a permanent abode. So they tried to attach themselves to a household. Shakespeare's company had found a noble patron in one of the Queen's favourite courtiers, Lord Leicester. The first record of Lord Leicester's Men dates from 1559, five years before Shakespeare was born. In 1560, they played before the Queen at Christmas. From 1570 onwards, they were often to be found playing at Court, so it was not surprising that when the Queen's own company was formed in 1583, many of Leicester's Men were incorporated into it. For some years the different companies in England formed and reformed. But at the accession of King James I in 1603, Shakespeare's company were at once invited to become the King's Men, a clear indication of their high status and reputation.

Apart from being an established company, the most stabilising achievement for this company was the construction of the first purpose-built theatre in England. They built it outside the City of London, because, despite the popularity of plays at Court and amongst the citizens and visitors, they were not allowed to perform within the city walls. City officials were uneasy about the social unrest (rioting and hooliganism were not unknown), and about the danger of plague spreading in places of public gatherings. Some officials were Puritans, who disapproved of plays, players and playgoers.

The first theatre was built in 1576 in Shoreditch. It was later dismantled and reconstructed south of the river, on Bankside in Southwark, where it was called The Globe and housed the first performances of many of Shakespeare's plays. His company also acquired a private theatre within the city walls at Blackfriars. It was smaller, more elegant and less frowned upon by the City officials. Often, the company still went on tour, but now they had somewhere to return to, somewhere to store costumes and scenery, somewhere to rely on a regular source of income, instead of simply passing round the hat. In acquiring property, too, they were increasing their capital. Shakespeare, the actor Richard Burbage, and his brother Cuthbert, were among the shareholders of The Globe. The theatrical profession was, for the first time in England, financially independent.

The number of actors at The Globe was much smaller than the cast needed for the great Corpus Christi plays. There were fifteen or twenty in the company, including boys and youths to play the women's parts. New plays were needed all the time to bring in the audiences. Shakespeare wrote thirty-three plays within about twenty-five years, as well as being an actor. Often the same costumes and props could be used, but still the plays had to be learnt, and any production problems solved. New plays were staged almost every week, while the most popular ones were frequently revived. Other theatres opened during the same period: The Rose, The Swan, The Hope, all on Bankside, as well as other private ones within the City. Yet the appetite for play-going was great enough to keep them all in business.

When theatre is offered as a general pastime, not as a seasonal or occasional celebration, publicity is necessary. In London, word-of-mouth was probably the most successful method of spreading the news, especially when the habit of play-going was well established. London theatre enjoyed a national and international reputation, then, as now. Visitors from all over Britain and Europe joined the citizens to flock across London Bridge to the entertainment centre on Bankside. Outside London, actors announced their arrival with a procession and band through the town, publicising their presence and programmes. Only in a later period would printing be cheap enough to warrant playbills and posters. When it came to Court entertainment, the preparation and organisation required an officer to supervise the work. The post of Master of the Revels at the Tudor and Stuart Court was comparable with the grandest of impresarios.

Professional theatre must inevitably compete with other kinds. The success of Shakespearean theatre was so great that it ousted much of the seasonal and community theatre which had sown the seeds of the English tradition. There was a clash between the people at Court, who thoroughly enjoyed theatre, both to watch and to participate in, and the Puritans, who heartily disapproved. It came to a head in the religious and political disputes which led to the English Civil War. When the Royalists were defeated in 1642, the theatres were closed, until the Restoration of Charles II in 1660. But even that gap, during which some undercover theatrical activity persisted, did not dampen enthusiasm for the professional theatres, which reopened their doors in triumph and began the unbroken tradition that continues even now. So strong was the English and European tradition of commercial theatre that, by the end of the nineteenth century, it seemed to dominate the world. Colonialism had spread its influence far and wide. Let us examine its growth.

Development of the theatre industry

In many parts of the world, the kind of theatre described up to now has appeared, in various forms and at various times. Seasonal and communal theatre, itinerant entertainers, professional theatre centring on the Court, on the households of great lords and ladies, and in the towns and cities. You can trace its history in relation to the changes in prosperity, the styles of governments and their attitude to the arts in each country or state, varying from the most oppressive regimes imposing censorship, to the most liberal. The attitude of the established religion towards the theatre has always affected it. War, civil strife and other disasters obviously have their effect too. Also, theatre, the most fleeting of the arts, has been particularly vulnerable to the whims of fashion. At various times it has been considered a vulgar pursuit, suitable only for the poor and uneducated sections of society, while at other times it has become a pastime for the elite, which the mass of the population finds either too expensive or too refined to enjoy. It is necessary to consider all these factors in examining the history of theatre in any one place.

In the nineteenth century, a new shaping force affected the theatre of Europe, in the form of the Industrial Revolution. When the railways were built, the whole pattern of theatre changed. Companies could travel all over the country in a matter of hours, with large quantities of scenery and costumes. But the changes went further than this. With the beginning of mass production as a new method of manufacture, came the idea of the industrial entrepreneur as a new kind of producer. Even before cinema, radio and television entered the field to rival live entertainment, the business of theatre changed in response to a changed attitude to work, leisure and money.

In mid-Victorian England, as in other parts of Europe and in North America, professional theatre had been mainly organised and performed by companies perhaps no bigger than Shakespeare's, though the lavish entertainments offered at some large theatres required many supernumeraries or extra performers. The manager of the company was often the main actor, the repertoire built round his or her talents. Before the coming of the railways, supporting actors were attached to a theatre on a semi-permanent basis, especially in the provinces. Star actors might travel from one town to another, allowing a couple of rehearsals only for the stock

company, as it was called, to be fitted into the production, with the help of a stage manager to coach. The performances must have varied from the sublime to the ridiculous, but no one expected them to be all the same. But when the railways came, whole companies could be transported round the country, with scenery, costumes and props. Instead of having only the script and the main actors as constant factors, the entire production could be reproduced. Against the competition of touring companies, the stock companies began to dwindle. Many provincial cities were soon without a local resident company which could offer a variety of theatrical entertainment, with or without a visiting star.

In London, New York and other big cities, a change also occurred in the variety of plays offered. Plays had usually been presented in repertory, that is, a number of plays that were in the repertoire of a company were offered at any one time, the programme changing from night to night. New productions were added, old ones dropped, perhaps to be revived later. Classics, popular successes or original plays made up the repertoire. Actors had little chance to get stale, with an ever-changing bill. But gradually this repertory system was replaced by a run, that is, the mounting of one production at a time, non-stop, until there was no audience left. This system suited the new entrepreneurial spirit which was inspiring America and Europe. As with the Ford motor car, you designed a product, manufactured a prototype, then reproduced it as long as the market would stand it. Show business began, with the entrepreneur sometimes playing little direct part in the production. Property speculation also entered the theatre business. Formerly, most theatres had been built, owned and/or managed by theatre people, keeping that close link with the building which Shakespeare's company had first established in England. Now it was broken. Rents in the capital cities soared, so that before a production could be mounted, investment had to be sought. The commercial theatres on Broadway, New York, and in the West End of London, now existed first and foremost to make money rather than theatre. Then when the entertainment industry found more profitable markets in movies and television, the live theatre became a poor relation.

The effect of commercialising theatre was to break up the

established companies; if each production was to be mounted separately, it was obviously more efficient to select the play, the actors, designers and production team separately too., The productions themselves were more highly polished. Where rehearsals had once been rushed affairs conducted by the stage manager or the leading actor, it became common practice to rehearse for several weeks under the direction of a producer or director. Scenery and costumes were no longer taken from stock, but designed and created especially for each production. Marketing and publicity also became sophisticated. Commercialism raised the overall technical standard of theatre, but there were some losses.

The main loss was that the organisation of professional theatre was no longer in the hands of theatre people. The actor-manager, running his or her own affairs, largely disappeared. (In the novel *Nicholas Nickleby* Charles Dickens painted a lovable comic portrait of a Victorian theatre manager, in the character of Vincent Crummles.) As for the supporting actors, the gipsy life, always associated with the itinerant actor, now affected the whole profession, who drifted from one job to the next, haphazardly picking up opportunities to train and perform, relying on the offices of an agent, a new figure in the theatre profession, to help find them work. Like other professions/trades, the theatre finally sought protection and solidarity through trades unions.

Theatre in the modern world

As we saw at the beginning of the chapter, theatre events nowadays can take all kinds of different forms. In both indigenous and immigrant cultures, ritual and religious theatre events continue to be performed. In some places their continuation may have been threatened by mass communication and the sophistication of modern culture; but now, the combination of local pride with the interest of anthropologists and the fascination of tourists often ensures their survival. There is a danger that such performances become purely theatrical entertainment, out of touch with the deeper purposes behind them. In Bali, for example, participants in traditional theatre practices often have to protect their private rituals from the prying eyes of tourists;

while in America, Indians may be persuaded to perform a rain dance whose meaning they have half forgotten, for the amusement of tourists and to earn a few dollars. In European cultures, archaic drama survives too; for example, in children's games and in rituals performed at Hallowe'en and other special occasions, and in village performances such as the Polish Herod play.

As for the great festivals of drama, a romantic desire arose in the nineteenth century to revive such events, a desire increased by more widespread knowledge of theatre history. In Germany, in the late nineteenth century, the composer/dramatist Richard Wagner yearned for the all-embracing form of theatre he felt the Athenian and medieval European festivals had been. In 1876 he founded the Bayreuth Festival, where his operas are still performed annually. A Salzburg Festival was founded in 1917 in honour of Mozart. In Britain, the biggest modern festival is at Edinburgh and was founded in 1947 as a Festival of Music and Drama; while in York, the first modern revival of the mystery plays took place in 1951. Many other revivals have followed. The most continuous tradition of Christian drama is at Oberammergau in Upper Bavaria. There, during a plague epidemic of 1633, the villagers made a vow, in supplication for recovery from the sickness, to perform a passion play every ten years. Beginning in 1634, they have faithfully performed it at ten-year intervals almost without exception.

Many other modern festivals exist all over the world, gathering the arts together in one city or centre for several days or weeks. Often a sense of celebration is achieved, but it does not always involve the whole community. The greatness of the Corpus Christi plays and the City Dionysos in Athens was based on a strong combination of sacred and secular celebration. In both these events, the worship of the god (Christ or Dionysos) was linked with the cycle of the seasons; the death and resurrection of both these gods also meant, at some level of consciousness, winter and spring. The cities were sophisticated and proud enough to mount a lavish and complicated event, but were still closely connected with the agricultural year.

Replacing the patronage of monarchs and nobility, governments and other national or local organisations now

fund many theatre events, aiming to show the best of past and present plays and productions. Businesses too, as well as individual wealthy citizens, will often choose to fund a theatre event, seeing it as a significant way of visibly benefiting the community. Old theatrical traditions are cherished, such as the unique Japanese *Noh* theatre, which almost died out in the nineteenth century but now has an established, though specialised, audience.

In the great cities of the world, much Westernised commercial theatre is performed, with paler imitations in the smaller towns. Alongside it, alternative forms of theatre emerge, often combining elements of Western, Eastern and Third World traditions in new ways. Theatre in educational institutions sometimes opens the way to more experiment. In Africa, for example, universities such as Ibadan in Nigeria are at the forefront of theatrical development.

All in all, theatre events are much more varied than a glance down the entertainment column of a newspaper might lead one to think. They are happening in and out of theatre buildings all over the world. Whenever you see or hear about a theatrical event, large or small, give some thought to who is organising it, why, when, and where it is happening, how you heard about it, and who, if anyone, is paying for it.

3

Theatre space

THEATRE events take place in real time and real space. The performers are as real as the audience, unlike those on film or video, who are represented by light and dark on a screen. In this chapter we examine the different kinds of space used for theatre.

Features of the space

The first requirement of a theatre space is that it should allow people to gather round to watch and hear the performers. The word 'round' gives us a clue to one of the commonest arrangements of space, the circle. The circle shape is basic to group communication. Huts in a tribal village are often built round an open central space, while within the hut itself the family may gather round the fire in the middle. Folk dances and children's games often take place in a circle, with or without some participants in the middle.

A circle divides those inside from those outside. Many games and rituals are based on the crucial step inside or outside the circle. The marking of a circle on the ground, whether it is done by a simple chalk line, or by an arrangement of stones, is often endowed with a magical or sacred meaning. The circle of stones at Stonehenge, for example, is associated with ancient rituals. Theatrically, a circle is a useful device for distinguishing between performers and spectators. There may not even be a physical barrier, just a ring of spectators standing around the empty space in which the performance is taking place. A circle has a socially equalising effect on those around it. King Arthur's legendary Round Table was based on the idea that all his knights were of equal rank. For an audience arranged in a circle, there are no positions that are better or worse, even though those in the inner ring may have a better view.

Examples of simple circular performance spaces include the following, (described in *The Seven Ages of Theatre* by Richard Southern):

(1) English Mummers plays which include lines such as 'Ring a ring I enter the or', 'or' perhaps corrupted from 'orbit'.
(2) Tibetan festival drama in which the spectators form a large circle around a canopied acting area.
(3) Medieval stone rounds, of which one remains in Cornwall, plus illustrations of others.
(4) Aztec flying dance (preserved since pre-Christian times) in which *voladores*, flying dancers, swing out on ropes from a central pole.

A development of circular entertainment spaces can be seen in the circus tent and the boxing ring. The kind of entertainments best suited to a circular space are shows of physical display, especially when the outcome is uncertain. Then the tension and suspense (who will win the fight? will the trapeze artists succeed?) link the audience like an electric circuit. Often, a round theatre space is enjoyed in modern theatre because it encourages this sense of a shared experience.

Performance within a circle

It is often referred to as arena staging, because the audience is on all sides, as in a sports arena. For spoken plays, however, a complete circle is, in some ways, an inefficient shape for performance, because the actors must always have their backs to a part of the audience. In moments when the drama requires that attention be paid to one actor, when the actors' faces must be seen, or when an actor needs to be in a commanding position, then being inside a circle may not be effective. Therefore, a more common arrangement for doing plays, is for the audience to arrange themselves, or to be arranged, in a partial circle, leaving one section free for the actors. Such an arrangement gives the actors a dominant position, especially if they are raised above the audience.

We shall look at some of these partial circle arrangements when we come to examine theatre buildings. First, let us consider another shape, the rectangle, which often occurs when some kind of construction is involved, such as a platform or building. Outdoors, courtyards have often been used for theatre space; indoors, rectangular rooms and halls, though not perhaps the ideal shape for theatrical performances, have nevertheless often been used and adapted.

In Spain, the courtyard or *corral* was the regular space for theatre events. In India and in many other parts of Asia, rectangular temples housed theatrical performances, or formed the basis for the design of theatre buildings. In Tudor England, the inn-yard was a good place for public entertainment, being a natural gathering point for travellers and townspeople. It was designed around a central courtyard, with archways at each end, through which carts and wagons could pass. The common rooms were on the ground floor, the bedrooms above, with open corridors running around on both levels. Plays were presented in the open inn-yard, on a platform, with spectators standing around it, while some more favoured people watched from the galleried passage-ways above.

For indoor entertainment, halls of state, guildhalls and banqueting halls were useful spaces. It was often on feast-days that a monarch or noble required entertainment, when his or her subjects and guests were already gathered together for a banquet. They were seated or standing in places appropriate to their social position, with plenty of space

Performance in a hall

through which servants could pass, carrying dishes to and from the kitchen. The seating arrangement in a Tudor hall was much as it is today at many formal banquets. The master or mistress of the occasion sat in the middle of the top table, flanked by the most important guests and members of the household. The other tables were set longways down the room, the seating order descending in social rank away from the top table. (Hence the expression 'below the salt', the salt being placed half-way down, so those below it were the least important guests and household members.) This arrangement lent itself well to theatrical performance, with the audience seated or standing on three sides. There was often a screen between the hall and the kitchens, with doors that created natural exits and entrances for the actors. (In the play *Fulgens and Lucrece*, printed in 1515, the actors pretended to be household servants, and the transition from feast to play was part of the comedy.) Another advantage was the minstrel's gallery above the hall, so that music could always be an integral part of the entertainment.

In France, during the same period, players began to use indoor tennis courts for plays. Tennis was a rather different game from modern lawn tennis, but it too required a rectangular court divided into two halves. In these narrow buildings, a platform for the actors was set at one end of the room, while the audience sat in straight rows facing it. This more confrontational arrangement is typical of any long hall used for plays. It can be found now in old school-, village- and church-halls, and in other meeting-places. In this kind of rectangular arrangement it is easier for the actors to create the illusion that they are in a separate world especially if the platform is filled with scenery (see Chapter 7). The arrangements illustrated have formed the basis for many theatre designs in Europe. You will find that most are based on a circle, or partial circle, or on a rectangle, or on a combination of these shapes.

A theatre space has to fill two important functions. The first is that everyone must feel united in one spot, like a church congregation or people at a sports event. The second is that the performers must be visible and audible to as many of the audience as possible. To help fulfil these functions, variations in levels have been used. A raised platform for the actors immediately makes them visible to more people than the level ground. Alternatively, spectators are often perched above the stage, in boxes, galleries or on tiers which slope up, away from the stage. Many of these variations depend on the size of the theatre space, and the number of performers and spectators. For a small fringe theatre, a few rows of seats may be enough, arranged round the edge of a room, with perhaps one row raised on rostra. For a village drama, the level ground may be enough, with onlookers grouped around, peering through heads to get a better view. The English director, Peter Brook, took a company of actors through African villages, using only a floor-covering to define the stage area.

Sometimes, however, accommodation is needed for several thousand spectators. Social rank may require that some people have a better view than others. For example, in the Banqueting Hall at Whitehall, in London, the best view was from a central position, towards the back of the room, and there the throne was placed. Sometimes the social aspect of theatre-going is the most important. For example, in classical Chinese theatre, the audience sits at small tea-tables opposite each other, while in modern American dinner theatres, catering arrangements also have to be considered. In many European theatres, boxes and seats were arranged to give fashionable people a good view of each other, rather than of the stage.

So the nature of a theatre space is defined by its shape, levels, size, number of people to be accommodated and the social function it has to serve. Another interesting aspect is the actor/audience relationship the theatre space sets up. When a theatre space is improvised in a room, or in an open space, performers and spectators may be barely separated. Many rectangular spaces, however, divide the spectators from the performers, perhaps divide the spectators from each other. For example, one common modern form of rectangular staging is traverse, where the spectators are placed on two sides of the stage, confronting each other, like members of parliament in a debating chamber.

Some forms of theatre make use of a raised walkway, along which performers can enter, above the spectators, yet almost mingling with them. In Japanese *Kabuki* theatre, such a walk-way, called the *hanamichi*, or flower way, connects the back of the auditorium with the front of the stage. It is rather like the kind of walkway used in fashion shows, which juts out either down, or across, the room. Many variety theatres, such as the *Folies Bergères* in Paris, have included a walkway along which performers can parade, then return to the main stage.

In the theatres of Ancient Greece, most of the spectators were above the performers, seated in a fan-shaped auditorium which was carved out of the natural curves of the hillside. The stage still dominated the space. Common features can be found throughout the world, where spaces have been created for a theatre event, yet new variations still remain to be invented or discovered. A Russian director, Nicolai Okhlopkov (1900–67), experimented with many different arrangements of stage and auditorium, including putting the spectators in the middle, while the drama was unfolded around them; and using several different stages around or above the spectators. Yet his innovative ideas had much in common with earlier forms of staging.

A most unusual form of raised staging is used in a traditional Indian performance called *Khyal*. The action takes place on a central platform, while two smaller ones are used

Staging *Khyal*

for singers and instrumentalists. Two high platforms are used as dressing-rooms. The actors enter, females from one side, males from the other, down the ladders, singing their lines. In another Indian play, the acting area is divided into twenty-one sections arranged like the petals of a lotus flower.

Temporary theatres

At the beginning of Anton Chekhov's play *The Seagull* (first performed in Russia, in 1896), the hero, Konstantin, was constructing a stage for the performance of a play he had written. It was a simple wooden platform, with curtains in front. His family and friends sat in front of the stage, on chairs and benches gathered from the garden and the house. When the curtains were pulled back, the lake behind the stage created scenery more beautiful than any he could have made. But his play was interrupted and never performed. The last act of *The Seagull* took place two years later. The remnants of the stage were still there, flapping in the wind on a cold wet winter's night. It was a melancholy, desolate image. Nothing is sadder than an empty theatre. Perhaps that is why actors have so often been content to perform in temporary theatres, swiftly constructed as a circus tent is pitched, to be taken down and carried away afterwards.

One simple form of temporary theatre is a booth stage, consisting of a platform and curtains, set up in whatever convenient place presents itself – at a fair, in a market-place, an inn-yard, in front of a church or temple – wherever an audience can be attracted and gathered round. Variations on the booth stage abound. It may be mounted on trestles or barrels, or on wheels, so that strolling players can use it on their travels. It may have extending flaps, so that a larger stage can be built. A trap-door can be built into it, and/or a roof added.

Throughout the world, and throughout theatre history, some kind of booth-stage has existed, and does exist, as a form of portable theatre. What it achieves, more than the simple clearing of a space does, is a bigger sense of the actors' presence. The setting up of the platform, or the arrival of a wagon which unfolds into a stage, creates an anticipatory excitement which is good publicity for casual

A booth stage

performers. Although the acting space on a booth stage must necessarily be limited, this is compensated by the advantage of height which the raised platform gives, providing better viewing and more focus. The curtains give the actors the opportunity for variety and surprise. Costumes and props and actors can be concealed and brought out quickly, when they are needed. More open staging, in contrast, has to show its hand, either having everything in view, or having exits and entrances through the audience, or beyond the stage area.

One of the most elaborate uses of the booth type of stage was in the medieval festivals described in the last chapter. In England, France and other parts of Europe, the cycles of mystery plays were performed on a series of booth stages.

In York, where the Corpus Christi plays were wheeled through the streets, the stages were pageant wagons, each one carefully built to suit the appropriate guild play. In some towns, the stages were wheeled through the streets, then set up in front of the Cathedral, or in the town square or other suitable large space, grouped in a vast semi-circle. This space itself became a large theatre space, bounded by the pageants on one side and the audience on the other, perhaps separated by a fence. When the festival was over, the pageant wagons

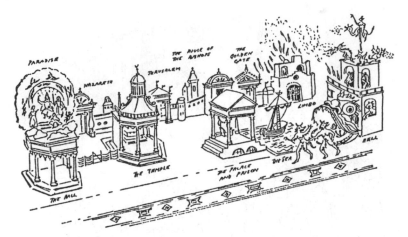

Stages for a mystery play

were wheeled away and stored for the following year. They were not so much temporary, as portable.

The need for permanent theatres

The need for a permanent theatre is created as much by the needs of the audience as by the needs of the actors. While permanent theatres may allow for greater comfort for the actors, and greater sophistication in the production, a very important function is to contain the audience within a space that allows the actors to control their attention. This idea of containment is also extremely important economically. If the audience is expected to pay admission, then there has to be a clear demarcation of territory. We shall therefore examine three ways in which control of the audience has influenced the creation and design of permanent theatres:

(1) The audience must be able to see and hear.
(2) Their entrance and exit must be monitored, and perhaps also their position and behaviour inside the auditorium.
(3) There must be maximum facilities for controlling their imagination.

These then, are the chief concerns in constructing permanent theatres.

Seeing and hearing

It is just as important to hear a play well, as to see it well. Those who attend a play are called an audience and where they sit or stand is called the auditorium, both words deriving from the Latin word meaning 'to hear'. Although nowadays we speak of going to *see* a play, it has been just as common to *hear* a play. In reality, both faculties are needed, but some kinds of plays are more of a spectacle than others. We have already noted that all-round seating is often more suitable for a spectacle than for a play, and this is partly because of the acoustics.

When we consider how the audience is to hear well, we probably think first of all of distance. Those nearest the actors will hear best, and there is a limit beyond which an actor cannot be heard. While this is true in very broad terms, it has to be modified by other factors. Visitors to the Ancient Greek theatre at Epidauros are treated to the experience of its quite remarkable acoustics. An actor on the stage who whispers, or who drops a single coin on the ground, can be heard distinctly from the furthermost seat, which is hundreds of feet away. The science of acoustics is still imperfectly understood, but this theatre, scooped out of a hillside, has a cave-like quality which directs and contains the sound. Modern methods of amplifying sound electronically have their beginnings in more rudimentary kinds of amplification, including modification of the shape and proportion of the theatre, use of materials that conduct sound well or, in other places, materials that are soundproof, and methods that a skilled actor can use to project and amplify his/her voice.

The theatres in Ancient Greece were all outdoors. Some compensation for the diffusion of sound was provided by the actors wearing masks, which channelled and amplified the sound of their voices. It is nevertheless surprising that a theatre can hold an audience of thousands, and still have every sound audible. Audibility can be lost by the sound being directed away from the audience, or through too much distracting sound, or through an actor's lack of skill. There are also occasional dead spots to be found in some theatres, places where, for no reason that can be discovered, the voices from the stage simply do not reach adequately.

Hillside theatre in Greece

For the audience to *see* well, distance is, again, an important factor, but there are other considerations as well. Geometry can discover the sightlines, that is, whether or not each member of the audience has an unobstructed view of the stage. One of the most effective designs for creating good sightlines is, again, the fan-shaped auditorium to be found in many Greek and Roman theatres. The Greek theatres were often carved out of a hillside, rows of stone seats being hewn out of the rock, while the later, Roman ones were built from scratch, in imitation of the Greek. In the rest of Europe, and in the East, this fan-shape was not used. In the nineteenth century, Richard Wagner, already mentioned in Chapter 2, was inspired by the comprehensive nature of Greek theatre. In his theatre at Bayreuth, he imitated the sweep of seats fanning out round the Greek stages.

Both European and Eastern societies incorporated into their theatre designs a greater consciousness of social status. From the time of the Renaissance, the European auditorium developed with clear divisions between seating for the various levels of social and economic privilege. Another factor was the development of theatre-going as a social activity. Until the nineteenth century, in European city theatres, it was just as important, if not more important, to *be* seen, as to see. Until Wagner built his theatre at Bayreuth, it was not customary to darken the auditorium. In classical Chinese theatre, theatre-going is a social activity, often with eating and drinking going on, so that the focus is not directed solely towards the stage.

Coming in and out

When we come to the second way in which the audience is controlled, their entering and leaving, and their general deportment, the social and economic position of the theatre-goer is also important. In European city theatres, from the sixteenth to the twentieth century, the rich and powerful members of society have been seen to have the best seats. Entrance into the theatre has therefore not been by general admission, but to particular sections or seats. The way to better parts of the house has been barred as securely as the way from steerage to first-class on a passenger ship. However, different sections of the auditorium have at different times and places been considered the *best* seats. In the early European public theatres, the area near the stage was often left for standing room, or for cheap benches; but during Victorian times, the general comfort of the auditorium was improved, and the ground level was filled with comfortable and expensive seats.

Controlling the imagination

Now we come to the stage area, from which the actors affect the minds and hearts of their audiences. We have seen already that various spatial relationships have been used between the stage area and the auditorium, whether or not the theatre is purpose-built. Now let us look at the stage area in more detail.

First we consider the actors' background. Although a stage surrounded by audience on all sides is possible and often powerful, players have more often taken advantage of any arrangement that gives them a special background, especially if it allows for entrances and exits into and out of the audience's view. A wooden screen, as in the Tudor hall, and

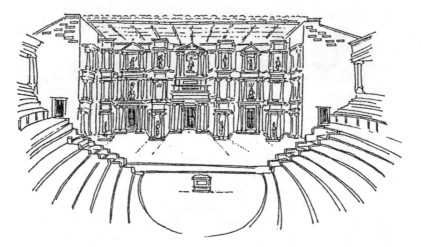

Façade of a Roman theatre

the Chinese theatre, a stone façade, as in Greek and Roman theatres, a curtain strung across a booth stage; all these provide early models for the façades built into later theatres, behind the platform on which the players performed. Scenery could be placed in front of the façade, though it was also placed behind. In fact, changes in use of that scenic background, and the actors' position in relation to it, are an important part of the story of European theatres, as they developed from the Renaissance to the nineteenth century.

In Eastern theatre, the provision of scenic background has never been as important as in Europe. In India, where theatres may have existed as early as 200 BCE until about 500 CE, a curtain bisected the stage into the acting area and the backstage space. In China, where many theatre buildings existed during the Sung Dynasty (960–1279), then were less common until the eighteenth century, the background seems always to have been a simple wooden screen with plain doors cut into it, and embroidered hangings. In Japan, the first theatres for the *Noh* drama developed in the fourteenth century. The background was, and still is, a screen with a tree depicted on it, reminiscent of the open air shrines where *Noh* drama originated.

The second spatial feature to consider is the division between the acting area and the auditorium. The actors may

Tree screen of the Noh stage

be divided from the audience by the height of a platform, by
an orchestra pit, by a line of footlights, by a balustrade, by a
boundary of light, by a curtain or scene drop, or by none of
these. Conventionally, the actors are separated from the
audience, even if it is only by a line on the floor, a line that
could be real or imaginary. And the line may trace various
shapes.

As we have seen, most stages are based on the shape of a
circle or partial circle, or of a rectangle. Three of the earliest
forms of permanent theatres demonstrate the various
possibilities. The early Indian theatres, based on temple
designs, separated the stage and auditorium in a straight
line, creating three clear divisions in the theatre – backstage,
stage and auditorium. The early Greek theatres had a large
circle on floor level, called the orchestra, where dancing and
singing could take place. The audience fanned out around
about half this circle, leaving space for side entrances. This
was a kind of intermediary space. Behind it was a raised
platform for the chief actors, backed by a stone façade,
providing doorways. This was a kind of compromise between
a circular and a rectangular stage. The Chinese theatres of

the Sung Dynasty provided yet another arrangement, with a platform jutting out into the audience, who were ranged on three sides. This very common form of stage, often called a thrust stage, has become increasingly popular during recent years, as it gives more immediacy to a performance than do stages which are sharply separated from the auditorium.

There are many variations on these basic theatre designs. All depend on the understanding that the audience and the actors share the same space, and yet are separated. At any point they could, and sometimes do, mingle, or change places. Only when, for a safety check, a steel curtain is lowered between stage and auditorium, can we truthfully say that the actors and audience are physically separated.

Backstage and front-of-house

The areas beyond the stage and auditorium, though not so basic to the art of theatre, are nevertheless important parts of the design or conversion of space. The actors must dress and have somewhere to wait; the technical staff and their equipment must be housed; scenery and costumes may need to be stored and maintained; rehearsal rooms may be needed; and there may be offices as well. The work of creating theatre stretches far beyond the stage area, but it is usually kept firmly out of sight of the audience. Actors and theatre staff enter by the stage door, often much humbler than the front entrance which the public use, and guarded by the stage-doorkeeper who lets in only the privileged few. In the parts of the theatre where the public go, known as front-of-house, are the box office, perhaps vestibules and foyers, bars and refreshment areas, to enhance the theatre visit. Here, the audience is on show, while backstage hums with the private preparations for the performance.

Whether a theatre is converted out of a village-hall or market-square, or meticulously designed and planned by a skilled architect, the dovetailing of space for all the people and activities involved in theatre requires much ingenuity. To describe the different kinds of facilities that have been and are in use would take too much space. Yet there is often a fascination with seeing the backstage world of theatre, like seeing the kitchens where great banquets are prepared.

People enjoy touring such places as the National Theatre of Great Britain, walking along its so-called 'Yellow Brick Road', along which can go scenery to all three theatres. Others wait in vigil outside a stage door, to catch the star emerging, or try to gatecrash their way in to see the stage. But the stage door, the rooms, passages and stairways beyond, and the back view of the stage itself, may look surprisingly ordinary, and perhaps shabby, in contrast to the artificial and imaginary world created on the stage.

Theatre architecture in Europe

Theatre design, then, has been a significant branch of architecture, especially in Europe, where a tradition of theatre building began at the end of the fifteenth century, in Italy, and has continued unbroken to the present day. Each new theatre was based on a combination of new and old ideas, partly derived from the remains of Greek and Roman theatres, and also inspired by experience of many other forms of sport and entertainment, together with new perceptions about science and the arts, and new technology. Nowhere did theatre flourish more than in Shakespeare's England. None of the purpose-built theatres of this time survive, but scholars have traced many features of their architecture, and we can conjure up, and even physically reconstruct, the stages and auditoria where such plays as *A Midsummer Night's Dream* and *Hamlet* were first performed. From that starting point we can briefly explore the development and influence of Europe's theatrical architecture.

Shakespeare's theatres

Permanent theatres were first built in England during Shakespeare's lifetime and career, but it would be misleading to associate his plays only with purpose-built theatres. Leicester's Men, or the King's Men, for whom he wrote, continued to perform in the provinces when the London theatres were closed, touring to halls, inn-yards and market places. In the capital itself his plays were performed in several theatres, both public and private, and at Court.

The first theatre in London built from scratch was simply

called The Theatre. It was built in Shoreditch, north of the River Thames and outside the city limits, in 1576, by James Burbage, with his two sons, Richard, who was to be Shakespeare's leading actor, and Cuthbert. Public theatre was not permitted inside the City of London, so when the lease on the Shoreditch land expired, James Burbage looked next towards Southwark, south of the river, and found, on Bankside, in the Liberty of the Clink, a perfect site controlled not by the City authorities but by the Bishop of Winchester. He and his sons had The Theatre secretly dismantled and carried across the river, timber by timber, where they re-erected it in 1599 as The Globe.

There were other theatres on Bankside by then – The Rose, The Swan, and The Hope. In fact it was a famous and lively entertainment area in the late sixteenth and early seventeenth centuries, with bear-baiting, bull-baiting, cock-fighting and brothels to entice the public across by ferry or London Bridge. Burbage and his sons were motivated by the desire to safeguard and consolidate their theatre business.

The Globe Playhouse and the other public theatres of the time were a unique phenomenon, both socially and architecturally. In designing and constructing a theatre, the master-builders employed on this and other projects had several kinds of model to inspire them. They used features of the inn-yards and Tudor halls already described, as well as the drawings and descriptions of classical theatres. The cockpits and bear-baiting rings also influenced them, as well as the booth stages and pageant wagons used by strolling players and guilds.

The Globe was a circular building in appearance, though actually made up of many straight sides. This circle consisted of a ring of galleries facing inwards on to an open yard, into which the platform stage jutted. Backing the stage was the tiring house, or dressing-room, with its ornate frontage, and with balcony and doorways leading on and off the stage. A trapdoor in the stage floor led to below the stage, this area perhaps being concealed from the audience by hangings around the stage. Above the stage was a glorious roof canopy, decorated with sun, moon and stars, to represent the heavens, and above that a kind of hut or lantern tower, from which such scenic pieces as a throne could be raised or lowered.

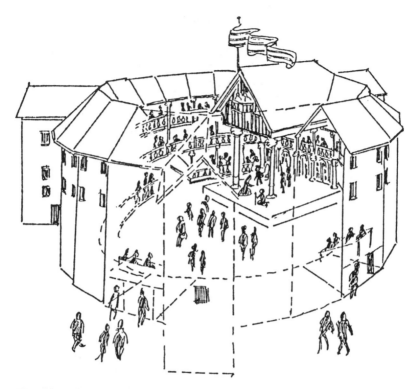

The Globe Playhouse

The theatre was thus partially roofed, with the yard open to the skies. This yard was therefore the cheapest area. Those who stood there were called the groundlings, and were drawn from the students, apprentices and common people, while the galleries were more expensive to enter, and housed gentlemen and nobles. Some privileged members of the audience may well have sat in the balcony overlooking the action. The idea of *being seen* at the theatre was already popular. This is the kind of theatre Shakespeare described in *King Henry V*, calling it 'this wooden O' and asking pardon for its simplicity. Like other public playhouses of the time, The Globe had little scenery. In many ways it resembled the early Chinese theatres, even though Shakespeare and his European contemporaries had no knowledge of their Eastern counterparts. But his company also used another playhouse,

The Blackfriars, where more complicated scenic effects were possible.

The Blackfriars was a private playhouse, that is, a smaller, indoor theatre, altogether more select than the large public playhouses. Private theatres were allowed in the City. The King's Men moved into The Blackfriars in 1609, using it as their winter home. Performances there were more sophisticated, taking place at night, lit by candles, whereas performances at The Globe were always by daylight, sun or rain falling indifferently on the spectators. Minimum admission to The Blackfriars was sixpence, six times the price of the cheapest entry to The Globe.

The Blackfriars was not purpose-built, but converted from a Great Hall. The whole audience was seated, either in rows at floor level, called the pit, or in the galleries and boxes that lined the long sides and end of the chamber. The theatre held about 700 people, while The Globe held up to 3000, yet the proportion and shape meant that the most distant spectators were further from the stage than anyone at The Globe. The basic shape was something like the early Indian theatres, and the tennis court theatres developed in France.

Shakespeare's company also performed at Court, where performances were lavish, given in the Banqueting Hall, which James I rebuilt early in his reign. It was shaped like The Blackfriars, with a throne of state placed at the end of the room for the king, and facilities for more complicated scenic effects. Court entertainments, organised by the Master of the Revels, were open only to invited guests and members of the household.

The Globe and The Blackfriars, where Shakespeare's company alternated their regular performances, pointed the way to two different kinds of theatre development. At The Globe, the audience gathered round a thrust stage, focusing on the immediacy of the actor's presence, and participating almost physically in the stage action. They represented a full range of social types, including nobles, artists, intellectuals, tradesmen and apprentices, tourists, vagabonds, servants, whores. At The Blackfriars, the audience was clearly separated from the stage, regarding the play in a more contemplative way. They represented the wealthier and more privileged sections of the community. Here, the whole art of theatre began to be elitist, lending itself to more lavish productions, including scenic effects. Theatre at Court was even more expensive and select. In Shakespeare's time, all these forms of theatre existed side by side, but by the middle of the seventeenth century, The Globe had disappeared. In England, and in other parts of Europe, aristocratic indoor theatres dominated the development of theatre architecture throughout the following centuries.

Court and city theatres

The flourishing of public theatres on Bankside and elsewhere, together with the popularity of theatre at Court, and the development of indoor theatres, reflected the growing prosperity of the business of London theatre in Shakespeare's time. This prosperity was paralleled in other European cities, such as Paris, Madrid, Florence, Venice and other North Italian towns. Other cities and countries followed, according to their political and commercial development. Gradually, in the seventeenth and eighteenth centuries, Dutch, Scandinavian and German cities joined those in England, France, Italy and Spain, in building playhouses during the years after Burbage's 'Theatre' in Shoreditch. Examples of theatres built in this period are: Teatro Olimpico in Vicenza, Italy, built 1580–4, designed by Andrea Palladio and based partly on designs of Roman theatres as described and sketched by the architect Vitruvius, whose works were translated into Italian in 1521; Teatro Farnese in Parma, Italy, 1620, one of the first theatres built for changeable scenery; Schouwberg theatre in Amsterdam, built in 1638.

For much of the period from 1600 to 1800, the theatres kept *out* more of the population than they attracted in. Patronised by the aristocracy, with the development of costly scenic effects much encouraged, these permanent theatre buildings in Europe reveal only part of the story of the theatre. Luxurious court theatres were built, to display the taste and patronage of some monarch, prince or duke. One such that survives is the elegant little theatre at Drottningholm, Sweden, completed in 1766 as a royal theatre for King Gustav III.

In London, the public theatres disappeared when the

theatres were closed during the Civil War. King Charles II
spent much of his exile in Paris. At his Restoration, in 1660,
he licensed two companies, both of which built indoor
theatres on the French model. The companies finally settled
on neighbouring sites in the West End of London, one in
Drury Lane, one in Covent Garden, where the Theatre Royal
and the Royal Opera House now stand. A new theatre
district was established. Still today the West End is the
centre of fashionable London theatre.

Both Drury Lane (first built in 1661), and Covent Garden
(first built in 1732), have been rebuilt at various times,
partly to accommodate a gradual increase in middle-class
audiences. This increase was paralleled in other parts of
Europe. As the great metropolitan centres grew, the
prospering middle classes enjoyed displaying their patronage
and wealth as much as the upper classes. One of the most
lavish theatres of this period was the opera house of La Scala
in Milan, built in 1778. Designed as a free-standing unit, it
had no less than five tiers or boxes, arranged in a great
horseshoe round the pit. The money for building such
theatres was raised by the sale or rental of boxes, or *loges*,
together with private retiring rooms. The pit was the cheapest
part of the house, just as it had been when it was an open
space occupied by groundlings, in Shakespeare's time. As the
illustrations show, these theatres combined curves and
straight lines, separating the stage not only by a raised stage,
but also by a framing arch which concealed its sides, or
wings. This arch was called the proscenium; it allowed a
complete stage picture to be built behind it. Proscenium
theatre dominated European theatrical architecture well into
the twentieth century.

Court theatres continued to be built in the eighteenth and
nineteenth centuries, to house operas, plays and ballets; and
large public indoor theatres were established in metropolitan
centres; but portable, temporary theatres had by no means
disappeared. Troupes of travelling players still toured in
Europe, though the records of their performances are scarce
compared with the large amount of scripts, accounting books
and theatre journalism which record activities in the major
theatres. In Italy and France, the touring players are
particularly linked with the *commedia del arte* tradition of

Proscenium theatre

improvisational acting, while in England, the growing popularity of Shakespeare's plays helped to foster a tradition of barnstorming, the name given to touring companies who performed in barns and who developed a ranting, violent acting manner. This tradition spread as far as Germany. In provincial cities, smaller public theatres sprang up, such as the Georgian Theatre at Richmond in Yorkshire, which still survives. But the establishment of permanent theatres had centralised the theatrical network. The aspiration of most actors, managers and playwrights was to rise from touring to provincial theatre, and from provincial theatre to the Court or city. The rewards of success were growing, in terms of money, fame and prestige.

Theatres and national status

The development of theatre in each Western country has varied according to its national fortunes and the local conditions, as indeed has theatre in all parts of the world.

The Northern Italian cities were important cultural centres by the sixteenth century. From the time of the Medicis in Florence, scenic and architectural splendour of theatrical presentation became an attractive way of displaying power, pride and wealth. By 1600 London and Paris were important centres too, and later, Amsterdam. But Germany, ravaged by the Thirty Years War which ended in 1648, saw little development of permanent theatres until the 1700s. By the 1800s the European style of theatre architecture had spread further afield. Royal patronage led the way towards *national* theatres, such as the Royal Theatre, Copenhagen (1772) and the Royal Swedish Dramatic Theatre (1788). In France, royal patronage of the Comédie Française made it virtually a national theatre too, and as such, it survived the French Revolution of 1789 with its prestige intact. In America, immigrants imported the European tradition and built theatres along the same lines. In Russia too, imitations of European theatre began in the early 1800s.

With this growing prestige and influence, it was not surprising that the European idea of theatre, linked inextricably with its permanent theatre buildings, came to achieve world dominance. In the nineteenth century, imperialism brought this form of theatre to Asia and Africa as well. For many people, therefore, what goes on in a proscenium theatre is still the clearest definition of what theatre is.

Yet as their empires expanded, Europeans also encountered other cultures. Although the Western style still dominates, the modern world has seen a fruitful mingling of many cultures, and nowhere more than in styles of theatre architecture.

Twentieth-century experiments

The theatres of the Renaissance were partly inspired by what their architects knew of Greek and Roman theatres. In the nineteenth century, too, men such as Richard Wagner were stimulated by knowledge of other kinds of theatres than the traditional eighteenth- and nineteenth-century models they saw around them. Following in Wagner's footsteps, many experimenters in the twentieth century have looked for new sources of design concepts in building theatres. They have rediscovered, for example, the qualities of the Bankside public theatres, explored the possibilities of Eastern theatres, found new parallels for theatrical entertainment in churches, sports arenas, circuses and fairgrounds. The variety of shape, size and scope in modern theatre design is vast.

For a sense of this variety, a selection of examples might include the following: Wagner's opera house, Bayreuth, 1876, Théâtre du Vieux Colombier, built in Paris, 1913, by the French director, Jacques Copeau, with a simple, architectural permanent setting on the stage; Grosses Festspielhaus in Berlin, built 1919–20, by Max Reinhardt, it was one of the first modern thrust stages, with a scenic stage as well; Theatre No 1914, a design for a theatre by the American designer, Norman Bel Geddes, a theatre in a dome, never built; Municipal Theatre in Malmo, Sweden, 1944, an adaptable theatre for thrust and/or scenic presentations; Playhouse Theatre, in Houston, Texas, 1950, a theatre in the round; Festival Theatre, Stratford, Ontario, 1953, a thrust stage designed by Tanya Moiseiwitsch for director Tyrone Guthrie, for a Shakespeare festival; Mermaid Theatre, in Blackfriars, London, 1959, a stage open to the auditorium; the National Theatre, London, 1976, consisting of Lyttelton (proscenium stage), Olivier (open stage), and Cottesloe (courtyard style).

A theatre is a house of dreams and fantasies. There is no kind of building that can serve all its purposes. For a limited period, or for a limited range of plays, one kind of theatre may meet the needs of actors, designers and audiences. The Elizabethan public playhouses had their day, the Japanese *Noh* stages help maintain a cherished tradition, the conventional European theatre dominated theatre architecture for several centuries, with its proscenium stage and tiered auditorium of stalls, circles and balconies. Nowadays, when a theatre is to be built, there is no simple answer to the question 'What should it be like?' When the National Theatre of Great Britain was opened on the South Bank in London in 1976, it was the fruit of many years of plans and rejected designs. To meet the flexible needs of modern theatre it was built with three different stages and auditoria.

Theatre conversions

You could say that any space used to put on a play has been
temporarily converted into a theatre, whether it is the open
space in a tribal village, the market place in a medieval
town, a hall, inn-yard or tennis court. Any meeting place,
from church to convention hall, can be used to mount a play.
Or a whole city could be turned into a theatre, as happened
in 1919 in Leningrad, when the storming of the winter palace,
which had happened the year before, was re-enacted in the
streets.

Where the natural conditions are right, as in the hillsides
around the warm Mediterranean, theatres can be created out
of the landscape itself, providing not only its own audiences
and actors with auditorium and stage, but leaving later
generations with a perfect model on which to base new
theatres. Around 1500 in Europe, that design inspired the
northern Italians, and then spread further north and west, to
England, France and Spain. The idea of creating a special
building for theatrical entertainment suddenly revived, after
centuries of portable theatre, temporary stages and hasty
conversion of existing spaces. For the next four hundred
years the European idea of theatre was dominated by the
developing form of theatre buildings, and it grew to dominate
other parts of the world. Now that dominance is breaking up,
and theatre is considered as an event, which might happen in
all kinds of spaces, rather than as a building. Despite a huge
number of theatre buildings still in existence all over Europe,
theatre companies often prefer to convert a non-theatre space,
such as a pub, a warehouse, a church or a gymnasium.
Economically, artistically and socially, such spaces may
better suit their purposes than an old-fashioned theatre. The
purpose-built theatre sometimes stands dark and empty, like
Konstantin's in *The Seagull*, until it is converted to a cinema
or bingo hall, while a lively youth theatre group provides
entertainment in some café basement.

4

Mask and costume

UNIQUE among all the arts, theatre consists in presenting human behaviour directly. How do we know, when an actor performs, that he/she is not behaving as him/herself, but as some other being? The borderline between what is theatre and what is real life is sometimes hard to distinguish. In fact, the excitement of theatre sometimes comes from not quite knowing. However, actors do need to be sure that the audience understands that they are *acting*.

You can see the importance of this if you think of a scene where a character commits a crime. The actor does not want to be held morally or legally responsible for that crime. To take another example, the character Juliet confesses undying love to Romeo, but the actress playing the part does not want to be accused of infidelity when she leaves the theatre with her real boyfriend. The *actor*, and the *character* he/she plays are not identical. In this chapter we address the questions – who is the actor? How do we know he/she is acting?

Actors often put on a disguise, changing their appearance from their normal selves. The effect of the disguise is, not only to present whatever character is being portrayed, but to protect the actor's identity, to signify to the audience that this is *acting* as opposed to real life. Since human beings express their thoughts and feelings most fully through the face, it has long been a theatrical tradition for actors to cover their faces with masks when performing. In Africa and in many parts of Asia, decorative masks are a striking feature of the performing arts, but in Europe, the mask has been much less important. Costume traditions have varied, too, from culture to culture.

African masks

Of all theatre traditions, the African tribal dramas and festivals are the least confined by buildings and limitations of space. Theatre remains close to its ritual roots. The making and wearing of masks are important ceremonial features. The masks themselves are significant works of art in their own right. Their use in ritual, drama and dance heightens and enriches theatrical experience. The study of African masks is a broad and varied subject, because each tribe and region has developed its own traditions. Here, it is possible only to point to the main characteristics of the art.

Being made of wood, tree-bark, grasses and other natural materials, the mask links the actor with the living world of which he/she is a part, especially when it represents an animal, or a symbol of growth and regeneration (such as the pregnant woman mask used in parts of Tanzania). It also links him/her with the world of his/her ancestors and the world of the spirits. The masks are cherished from one generation to the next, either by being carefully stored and used again, or by being physically destroyed and recreated on the same designs the next time they are needed. The masks are more important than the individual actors. They *are* the characters – of animals, spirits or members of the tribe, acting out dramas of life and death which affect all the people. The tradition and continuity which they represent are the force behind the energy and strength of African song and dance. They symbolise qualities of life and death which are important to the tribe. These masks often cover more than the face, concealing the whole body as well. This kind of disguise wipes out much of the actor's individuality. When you wear a mask, you find yourself expressing the quality of the mask, rather than your own particular thoughts and feelings. The mask itself is not designed to be a realistic imitation of what it represents. Indeed, how could one have a realistic imitation of a *spirit*? It is a decorative and symbolic representation. Significantly, appreciation of the primitive African masks has grown in the twentieth century, with the development of abstract art. But while African masks are associated with primitive art, the first great civic theatre tradition also used masks.

African masks

Masks for Greek drama

Masks in the Greek theatre

The Athenian drama festivals were among the first large social and religious theatrical celebrations. With complex organisation, and in purpose-built theatres, these festivals established the art of theatre in its own right. The masks of tragedy and comedy, typical of Ancient Greek theatre, are so well known that they are often used as the symbol of the theatrical art. Perhaps because of their priestlike function, actors in Greek tragedy wore conventional robes that set them apart from the audience, and masks which covered the whole head. None has survived, for they were made of linen, cork or lightweight wood. Characters in tragedy were usually gods or high-born men and women. The mask increased the actor's dignity. In later periods, it was often bigger than his own face. This, together with heightened shoes, made him literally larger than life. Masks in comedy were sometimes birds, animals and insects. For the human characters, the mask exaggerated qualities that were to be ridiculed in the play, baldness, ugliness, gluttony, lust and so on.

In Africa and in Ancient Greece, masks were an essential part of theatrical performance. Yet in Western Europe, despite the influence of Greek civilisation, a tradition grew up in which the mask had less importance, a tradition in which the actor was more closely identified with his audience, with the performer presenting himself bare-faced. This tradition arose out of the Christian culture which has permeated Europe for over a thousand years.

Disguise and the Roman Catholic Church

In the Corpus Christi plays, described in Chapter 2, the actors were, for the most part, members of the community. You might think that they would make great efforts, therefore, to dress up and disguise themselves, so that the audience would forget they were watching, say, the local butcher playing the role of Christ. But the truth was the reverse of this. Throughout the time of the mystery plays, the Catholic Church sought to stress the immediacy of its message and the human qualities of Christ. The Church wanted to encourage the idea that Christ was part of mankind at the same time that he was its God. Therefore, in the art of the time, Christ, his mother Mary, and all the other characters in the story, were depicted in the costumes of the time, with realistic faces. In the same way, the actors in the mystery plays presented themselves as they really were, as citizens of York, Chester or wherever it was, to show that everyone was sharing in the drama of the story.

The Catholic Church encouraged another form of drama which also required little or no disguise, at least for its main actor. This was the morality play, which was a kind of dramatised sermon, exhorting its audience to repent, and to seek salvation. The hero was called Everyman, or Mankind, or some other universal name. He was to be as closely identified as possible with the ordinary human beings who made up the audience. A heavy disguise was inappropriate.

Thus the Catholic Church helped to establish a tradition of European theatre in which the actor and audience were closely identified. When religious drama was suppressed during the sixteenth century, the convention it had established still continued. An actor was seen as someone representative of the audience, especially the actor playing the main character. Shakespeare and his contemporaries strengthened this convention. Hamlet, explaining his view of theatre in the tragedy that bears his name, says that the purpose of acting is: 'to hold, as 'twere, a mirror up to nature'. In England particularly, disguise was kept to a minimum, and masks were associated with devils and with pagan folk customs which had survived into the Christian world.

Commedia del'arte

One type of European theatre which did use masks regularly, was the *commedia dell'arte*, a tradition developed from Roman comedy by Italian and French touring troupes who were in their heyday during the sixteenth and seventeenth centuries. They developed a set of such instantly recognisable characters that comedies could be improvised from the barest outlines, creating endless variations on the predictable traits of these stereotypes. The plays relied on fixed social and moral types; for example, innocent maiden, lustful old man, bragging soldier, mischievous servant, cheating doctor, miserly father,

Characters of the commedia dell'arte

scolding wife. They wore masks or half-masks which exaggerated their characteristics. Generations of actors grew up, died and passed on these perennial character stereotypes. Probably each character was originally based on a real person, carefully studied and imitated in an exaggerated form, until, like a cartoon or puppet character, they began to acquire a life of their own.

Contemporary with this European form of theatre, a quite different tradition was developing in Japan, the *Noh* theatre. This aristocratic form brought the art of mask to great refinement.

Masks in *Noh* theatre

Theatre traditions had developed in many parts of Asia, with Sanskrit drama in India, shadow puppets in Java and a whole classical theatre in China, but many of these cultures were isolated from each other. Japanese culture, in particular, was cut off from other cultures from the early seventeenth century until the nineteenth. It was ruled by the *shoguns*, the military dictators who were at the top of a hierarchical society in which the highest class was that of the *samurai* warriors. The novel, *Shogun*, by James Clavell, gives a vivid impression of a culture living by stricter codes of behaviour than the pragmatic, adventurous Europeans. The Japanese theatre reflected this greater strictness and discipline.

In Japanese art, much is expressed by what is left out, as well as by what is put in. We can appreciate this by considering its characteristic brush and ink drawings, in which great spaces are left empty on the paper, giving much greater significance to the marks that are there. We may also consider the form of Japanese poem called *haiku*, consisting of seventeen syllables, into which a complete observation about life is concentrated. Application, training and discipline are associated with the spiritual programmes of Zen Buddhism, and with the martial arts. Other features of Japanese culture are: the emphasis on ceremony, exemplified in the ritual of drinking tea; and the emphasis on symbolic meaning, exemplified in the art of flower-arranging, which consists of much more than the achievement of a pretty effect.

These analogies are important if they help us to get a feeling for Japanese culture, with its emphasis on ritual, ceremony, symbolism, economy and discipline; for these are the qualities of the most sophisticated form of theatre, which is called *Noh*.

Noh theatre was at its height in the seventeenth century, and still continues as a preserved historical tradition. The actors wear wooden masks which are meticulously carved from specially seasoned wood. Making the mask is an art in itself. The finest masks are treasured possessions, like a Stradivarius violin. The putting on of the mask is an important ritual in preparation for the performance. It is seen as containing within it the power which the actor will acquire in wearing it. The actor contemplates himself in the mirror, wearing the mask, and draws power from that contemplation. When the mask represents a god, the effect is even more powerful. In practice, the fixed mask is a more flexible tool for acting than one would think. It can adopt a variety of expressions. Connoisseurs of the art can detect the most subtle use. One could compare the use of the *Noh* mask

Noh masks

with the use of a weapon or piece of sports equipment. A Samurai sword, for example, is a rigid, unchanging piece of steel; a cricket bat is a chunk of willow wood. But a master swordsman, or a Test cricketer, can manipulate what is in his hands in a hundred different ways, so that it seems to become a different thing altogether. That is the nature of a fixed mask, too, when worn by a skilled actor.

There is a long training in acting with a mask. A boy actor first wears a mask at the age of about twelve or thirteen, in a solemn ceremony which initiates him into adulthood. He is then allowed to perform several mask roles. By fifteen he is ready to perform in a young woman's mask, in a supporting role, and later, in a main role. Later, he adds more roles to his repertoire. First, the mask of the powerful warrior, then more mature women's roles, gods and demons. Only when he is past sixty, will he be allowed to wear the mask of an old woman. The main categories of mask are the old and young men and women, deities, and demons or monsters. The progression from one category to another marks the increasing subtlety in interpreting the roles, and also the increasing beauty of the masks. It might seem strange that a beautiful mature woman would be played by a man in his fifties, but only an actor who has spent many years on the stage is considered to have the power and skill to evoke the full poetry of the role, and to use the subtleties of light and shade falling on different surfaces of the mask. Some roles are performed without a mask, but the actor still aspires towards wiping out his own individuality, and expressing an eternal and transcendent truth about the role. *Noh* plays, which are lyrical, and expressive of deep emotion, are performed in conjunction with *Kyogen* plays, which are comical, just as the tragedies in Athens were followed by a riotous satyr play. There are fewer categories of *Kyogen* masks than *Noh*: gods, spirits, human types (such as Grandpa, the Ugly Woman, the Nun), and animals (the fox, the badger, the monkey, the ox, the dog and birds). The *Kyogen* masks exaggerate for a comic and grotesque effect, while the *Noh* masks symbolise the essential traits of a role.

There is great variety, then, in the different conventions used by actors to present themselves in role. There are other uses of masks in theatre and other methods of disguise. Asian and African theatre, and also indigenous theatre traditions in America, Australasia and other places, have made great use of decorative make-up and body paint, while in Europe such decoration has had less importance. Nevertheless, the decoration of the human body is significant in every culture, and the use of disguise tells us much about the position of the actor in every society and community.

The status of the actor

An actor's position is both higher and lower than his/her audience's. In most countries, only the most renowned professional actors have been given prestige and respect outside the theatre. Some cultures, including Islam and Christianity, have openly condemned the art of acting, though the Catholic Church learned to use theatre for its own purpose. Outright moral condemnation is based on the belief that acting is a deceit, since the actor pretends to be something he/she is not. Another reason for treating actors with contempt is that a habitual actor has no identity of his/her own. If you can play a beggar one day, and a queen the next, it is not easy to claim a social position of your own. In Elizabethan England, professional actors were liable to be arrested as rogues and vagabonds. In the seventeenth century, the French actor and playwright, Molière, was buried outside consecrated ground, simply because of his trade. In China, even though theatre was immensely popular, and actors underwent a rigorous training, they were nevertheless placed near the very bottom end of the social scale, often living in poverty and squalor. In many societies, professional actresses have been classed as whores. While outright condemnation of actors is rare now, still only the most successful entertainers achieve status. In 1895, the Victorian actor, Henry Irving, became the first theatrical knight. He was also honoured with burial inside Westminster Abbey.

But although the status of a professional actor has often been low, his/her position while performing is much higher. Actors have, by the very nature of their trade, far greater freedom of speech than ordinary people. We see this particularly in comedy. Whatever are the taboo subjects, such as sex and politics, the comedian can be more extreme in language and gesture, and can criticise his/her betters, because everyone understands that it is all part of the show. In order to exploit this freedom to the full, the comedian and the clown have often chosen to wear an extreme disguise than marks them out – a funny nose, or hat, or a white face. This is a long-standing tradition which goes as far back as the jester often attached to the court, whose job it was to entertain a monarch or noble, through song, mimicry and extemporised comedy. The character of fool or jester appears in several of Shakespeare's plays, including *Twelfth Night* and *King Lear*. The fool traditionally wore a motley or multi-coloured coat, like a harlequin costume. In fact the Harlequin character belonged to the same tradition. He was thus instantly recognisable as someone licensed to speak more freely, because of this special position. Often Shakespeare's fool characters speak frankly, even insolently, to their master or mistress, telling them truths that other characters could not speak unpunished.

Putting on a mask, or otherwise disguising yourself, is a method of protection from an audience who might otherwise hold the actor responsible for all that he does on stage, and for the lies that he tells. The disguise allows him to speak and act boldly. The protective quality of a mask is of psychological significance as well as being a theatrical convention; shy people can sometimes be persuaded to speak out without fear while wearing a mask. Yet the putting on of a mask or costume can do far more than protect. It can also bestow power. While this idea may be condemned as mere superstition, it is a superstition which has held powerful sway. Magical garments abound in fairy stories, conferring remarkable abilities on the wearer. In Shakespeare's play *The Tempest*, a magician deliberately relinquishes his magic powers at the end, and signifies this by taking off his magician's cloak. Priests in almost every religion wear special robes, and so do royalty. While this is partly so that people can recognise their special function, there is no doubt that the wearing of the robe also confers either power in itself, or a *sense* of power, which is virtually the same thing. Very few of us have not experienced what we might call the *Cinderella factor*, a moment when, like Cinderella in her ballgown, we felt the power of beauty or wealth by wearing the appropriate costume.

Use of costume

Actors put on costumes to give them power, as well as protection. There are also special objects used for the same purpose; for example, a wand, a jester's bauble, an orb and sceptre, a bishop's crozier. Theatrical costume, like ecclesiastical costume, has often been better than everyday wear. From the lavish displays in Renaissance courts, to the brilliance and elegance of *Noh* costumes, the magnificence of grand opera and the extravagance of a spectacular Broadway musical, audiences and actors alike have looked to costume to help create a feeling of enchantment in the theatre.

In the same way that masks have been a changing factor in the history of theatre, costume, too, has been used in different ways. Besides giving protection and power to the actor, costumes are also worn to show the audience what kind of a character is being represented in the story. While this may seem to be the most important function of disguise, it is in fact the most dispensable. A skilled actor can show character through his/her speech, movements and gestures. In this sense, then, disguise is an enhancement of the art of theatre, rather than an essential ingredient. Nevertheless, the use of costume, mask and make-up to show character is a fascinating subject of study.

In the European tradition, the development of character-costuming does not run altogether parallel with the development of costume in real life. This is because, while fashion changed century by century, decade by decade, stage costume changed in a different way.

We have already seen that the characters in the Corpus Christi plays were portrayed in a direct relationship with the audience. They were dressed in the same kind of clothes as the audience wore. The soldiers who hanged Christ on the cross in the *York Crucifixion play*, were dressed as they would be to fight for their own fourteenth-century lord or sovereign. Christ and the disciples wore simple robes, not unlike monks' habits and priests' vestments. When the Virgin Mary was raised up to the Queen of Heaven, her crown was a Gothic splendour. When it came to the morality plays already mentioned, the chief character, Everyman or Mankind or whatever he was called, had to be typical of whatever community the play was performed in, so that the audience could fully identify their own need to think of repentance and salvation. About him were grouped characters of a different kind. Often they were allegorical, that is, representing an abstract quality like Beauty, Fellowship, Mischief, Knowledge. They could usually be classed as vices or virtues, either hindering or helping Everyman's path to salvation. Since the dramatic aim was to alert the audience to the dangers and safeguards that could crop up in their own lives, costume had to reflect the audience's own community, with the character types clearly recognisable. We can get some idea of the sort of costumes they wore by studying the vivid pictures in manuscripts and churches. We can glean much from illustration to such books as Chaucer's *The Canterbury Tales*; there, the pilgrims each have a different place in medieval society, and are clearly distinguishable by their costumes. The tradition was thus established for European actors to wear appropriate contemporary costumes, with whatever adjustments were thought necessary. Those adjustments might indicate rank, profession, character type and moral value, exemplified in the vivid costumes of the *commedia dell'arte* troupes.

During the fruitful years when the *commedia* characters were flourishing, other forces influenced the development of stage costume. The rebirth of classical art, the Renaissance, starting in northern Italy, spread gradually west and north, bringing a consciousness of historical costume. Actors began to make some classical additions to their costumes if the play was a Greek or Roman story. Also, a split between tragedy and comedy became fashionable, with the costumes for tragedy becoming classical, ornate and dignified, while those for comedy remained a colourful reflection of contemporary society.

The development of expensive court theatre entertainments, also spreading from northern Italy, meant that the design of stage costume began to be an art in itself. In England, this phase reached its climax with the exquisite designs and costumes created by Inigo Jones, a near contemporary of Shakespeare, who contributed to the visual splendour of theatre, just as Shakespeare was contributing to its poetic splendour. His aim was to enhance and glorify reality, creating idealised figures out of legends, myths and allegories, far removed from the costumes of everday life.

This sophisticated style developed at the same time as the *commedia* troupes toured Europe with their robust, earthy, comic style. All these uses of costume in sixteenth- and seventeenth-century Europe had one simple belief in common, that the quality of a character could be revealed in his/her outward appearance. But in this rich period of theatre playwrights and actors were also keenly aware that people themselves played roles in life. The character of the hypocrite was developed, someone whose outward appearance belied his/her inner quality. The importance of this kind of character points to another reason why masks were used only to a limited extent in European theatre. An actor wearing a mask portrays a fixed character, and the mask helps him/her to express it, but a hypocrite is someone whose true character is

Designs for masques by Inigo Jones

concealed by the mask he/she wears. Molière's play *Tartuffe* (1664) was about the unmasking of a religious hypocrite. The character whom Tartuffe had duped exclaimed:

> What? Can it be that such a pious face
> Conceals a heart so false, a soul so base?
>
> (*Tartuffe*, Act v, Scene 1, l. 1602)

and was advised: 'Strip off the mask and learn what virtue means' (v, 1, 1622). The mask had become a metaphor, rather than a simple theatrical convention.

The conventions of European theatre costume were thus established, to continue well into the nineteenth century. Contemporary costume was worn, though fashion would make many alterations between the time of Richard Burbage, Shakespeare's leading actor, and later stars of the theatre, such as Thomas Betterton, David Garrick and Edmund Kean.

However, in the Eastern theatre, a different convention

Actors in eighteenth-century Europe

emerged, in which the decorative and symbolic use of costume was dominant.

Costume in the Eastern theatre

Sophisticated forms of Asian theatre originated in India. Chronology was not considered important in the Hindu and Buddhist cultures which developed there. It is therefore difficult to date the major early achievements of the Indian theatre, but it was certainly developed to a high level of sophistication by the early years of Common Era. At that time, a long treatise of dramatic art was written, the *Natya Sastra*, which was both a technical aid and a philosophical analysis, revealing much about the theory and practice of Indian theatre. The drama was closely associated with dancing. Troupes performing Sanskrit drama arose from the temple dancers who existed as early as 2500 BCE. Nowadays, traditional Indian forms of theatre survive in the *Kathakali* dancers, and also in dance/dramas performed in Burma, Thailand, Java, Bali and other parts of South East Asia.

Indian theatre emphasised the transcendental power of acting, the performers' ability to raise the audience's consciousness above the level of ordinary life to a spiritual awareness. The surface details of day-to-day living were not important in the theatre. Costumes, therefore, were not the clothes people wore every day, but decorative, ceremonial garments which symbolised the richness of spiritual life. The closest comparison with European costuming was the lavish, allegorical robes worn by actors in court masques. *Kathakali* dancers still appear in India, performing parts of the great mythical plays which were the basis for Sanskrit drama. They wear sumptuous apparel which bears little or no realistic or historical meaning. The bodice is lavishly decorated, and brilliantly coloured skirts are worn over their trousers. They wear huge, dome-shaped headdresses, sometimes with a kind of halo added, if they represent a god or goddess. They do not wear masks, but have a thick decorative make-up made of paste, which accentuates the appearance. There are five styles of make-up, each with its own colour scheme and design. Most male characters have long silver nails. The pupils of the eyes are reddened, heightening the dramatic

Kathakali dancer

expression and giving the performers a non-human appearance, as if they were dream characters from another world. When the art of theatre spread from India to China and other parts of Asia, this decorative and conventional form of costume was adopted, with brilliant displays of colour, texture and shape, enhancing the actors' appearance, and lending them a power and significance greater than their ordinary selves.

In Japan, the two traditional forms of theatre, *Noh* and *Kabuki*, are both associated with lavish, ceremonial costume which provides much visual appeal for the audience, and also reveals the significance of the characters. The costumes of *Noh* theatre are of a brilliance, elegance and luxury unparalleled elsewhere. Like those of the Indian dancers, they are ceremonial, bearing little relation to any realistic portrayal of the character. They are exquisitely made silken robes, deriving from the clothes of the court, the military nobility and the priesthood, but gradually constituting a distinct variety of dress, seen only on the stage. Woven in heavy brocades or translucent gossamer silks, the blend of colours, whether on the surface of the robes, between various layers, or between surface and lining, is breathtaking. The colours themselves, mainly white, red, light blue, dark blue, ultramarine, light green, russet, yellow ochre and brown, have symbolic significance. For example, red stands for youth, high spirits, good fortune; light blue for a quiet temperament; dark blue or ultramarine for strong roles; light green for menials; brown for old people. White is the colour of greatest dignity.

When the more popular form of theatre, *Kabuki*, developed in the eighteenth century, the display of brilliant costumes became an important part of that convention too. Make-up, wigs and costumes all evolved in such a way that the type of character being displayed could be identified by the audience as soon as the actor stepped on stage. Costume, in fact, became part of the action of the play. A change in personality or age of the character is shown by changes in costume taking place in view of the audience. For example, some characters pull off a sleeve of their outer garments when they

Kabuki actors

are stabbed, showing fabric beneath which signifies
something new about their character. Sometimes an entirely
new costume is revealed, by releasing the seams across the
top of the sleeves and letting a whole length of new cloth
appear. While these lavish and breathtaking displays were
being developed in Japanese theatre, in European theatre
such transformations occurred rather through the art of
scenery than of costumes. Instead, there developed in
nineteenth-century Europe, a new approach to costume,
which led to a greater contrast between Western and Eastern
theatrical conventions.

Realism and nineteenth-century Europe

As knowledge of science, history and geography increased in
nineteenth-century Europe, there grew up an awareness of
how environment affected character. It was no longer enough
to portray rank, profession, social and moral type through
costumes. The place and time to which the character
belonged took on an increasing importance. Modification of
normal dress no longer seemed appropriate costume for the
theatre. The period, environment and circumstances in which
the characters would have lived began to be researched, so as
to reconstruct the kind of clothes they would really have
worn. For example, for a production of Shakespeare's *King
John* in 1852, an attempt was made to reproduce authentic
medieval costumes, while for *Julius Caesar* a study of Roman
antiquity became necessary. The intention was to imitate the
period and location, clothing the character in costumes which
were historically and geographically accurate. The intention
was not completely carried out and never has been, because
each period perceives other times and places differently.
Even period costumes become dated, as we see from
Hollywood period films which bear the print of the decade in
which they were made, as well as the time the story covers.
For example, the nineteenth-century eye interpreted medieval
costume differently from the way we see it now. Individual
designers also interpret the visual evidence. Some will show
the dirt and squalor of the medieval period, while others will
emphasise its brilliant colours and ostentation.

The search for authenticity is easier to undertake in a

A nineteenth-century production of *Julius Caesar*

contemporary play. In the nineteenth century, many plays were written about the social problems of the time. Here, realistic costumes made an important contribution to the effectiveness of the production. Costume and make-up began to be more subtle and individualised. To portray the broad type, even in comedy, was not enough. It was no longer acceptable to enhance and decorate so as to make the visual effect pleasing. Indeed, costumes for realistic plays were often drab. Soon, the search for authenticity began to be a complicating factor when reviving an old play. Did authenticity mean you dressed the characters as they would have been seen at the time of the story, or at the time of the first production? Shakespeare presented interesting problems, because he had often written about times and places remote from his own time. Whatever solutions were found, certainly more effort was used to create costumes uniquely suited to a character in a particular play. The methods of research and reconstruction, whether for contemporary or historical costume, would later be transferred to design for cinema and television. Make-up, too, originally broad and heavy, especially in large theatres, gradually became more subtle, so that now, in film and television studies, and in some theatre companies, the art of make-up is as specialised as costume design.

The period in which authentic costume was being introduced, from about 1850 onwards, was also the period when the fictional world on stage was most clearly and physically separated from the audience (see Chapter 3). The whole environment was created on stage, with little reference to the audience, who sat in the dark. The off-stage area was hidden. Direct contact between actors and audience was minimal. The identification between the *actor* and his/her *character* became closer than the identification between the *actor* and his/her *audience*. Cinema and television took over the same convention, presenting drama so separated from the audience that the actors are not even present. The screen on which we see so much drama performed now, is a kind of substitute for the mask, for it too protects and enhances the actor, and also channels the performance into a concentrated form of expression.

Parallel traditions, East and West

The conventions of Eastern and Western theatre are most contrasted when we compare the *Noh* theatre, with its concentration on essential beauty, with the naturalism of European, and later American, theatre, with its detailed imitation of surface reality – 'warts and all'. The differences were perhaps most pronounced in the nineteenth century, just before the Shogunate ended in Japan, and cultural cross-fertilisation began. If we examine each tradition at a much earlier stage of development, greater similarities will be found. For example, the early *Noh* masks show more individualised faces than the later ones; the *Kyogen* traditional masks have some similarity to the European *commedia* masks; and the use of colour and pattern to convey symbolic meaning had great significance in medieval and Renaissance visual arts as well as in the East.

One aspect of mask, costume and disguise which has

featured in both traditions is transvestism, that is, adopting the costume of the opposite sex. In both Eastern and Western traditions, all-male professions grew up, with boys playing the parts of girls and young women, and men of various ages playing the older women's parts. Greater realism was nevertheless demonstrated in European theatre quite early on. In several of Shakespeare's plays, the heroine disguised herself as a boy, allowing the boy actor to look more convincing (*Two Gentlemen of Verona, As You Like It, The Merchant of Venice, Twelfth Night, Cymbeline*). The character sometimes drew attention to the double or triple role 'she' was playing, as a kind of in-joke with the audience. The actor in *Noh* drama was more closely identified by the audience with his woman-mask. He did not need any kind of apology, comic or serious, for being the opposite sex.

Kabuki theatre began when women were banned from the Japanese stage altogether. Its development was therefore closely associated with the skill of the female impersonators, the actors who adopted the *onnigata*, or female roles. Like actors for male roles, they undertook a rigorous training, progressing from young female roles to the mature women, and finally to the old women's roles. They presented an idealised kind of woman, as seen through the eyes of the men who played them, and strongly influenced by the moral attitude towards them.

In China, too, female impersonators were an important feature of the classical theatre. A characteristic of their performance was the imitation of the teetering way Chinese women walked when their feet were bound. Ironically, when actresses were allowed in classical Chinese theatre, in the twentieth century, they themselves had to learn how to do the female impersonators' imitations of walking on bound feet, even though that cruel custom was no longer practised.

In European theatre, women established themselves in the profession during the seventeenth century, and soon began their own role-reversals, taking on trouser roles, or breeches parts, especially in the eighteenth century. This convention was a conscious game with the audience, like the 'disguised heroine' of Shakespeare's plays. In Mozart's *The Marriage of Figaro* (1786) for example, one scene depended on a triple role, where a young man played by a woman was dressed up in women's clothes. In the traditional British Christmas pantomime, it is customary for a man to play the dame, and a woman the principal boy. These deliberate sexual innuendoes underline the European preference for acting to be a somewhat risky activity, rousing excitement by courting danger and disapproval, rather than leading the audience into a contemplative state.

Western and Eastern traditions have thus developed a variety of ways in which to use theatrical costumes and masks. One way could be called the 'theatrical hamper' approach: a group of actors delving into their colourful, miscellaneous stock, finding character masks, robes, hats, swords, aprons, crowns, gowns, beards, shirts, and so on. The fact that they are dressing up alerts the audience to the fact that a play is taking place. The actors select whatever is appropriate to the play and characters. Or a playwright or acting troupe may select characters and a story to suit the stock they possess. In some forms of theatre this stock approach has led to a strict system of roles, each with an appropriate costume, make-up or mask. A third approach is the creation of exotic, glamorous costumes which make a feast for the eyes and lift the audience into another world, either a pleasing fantasy, or a world of gods and spirits who are thought to influence men's lives. Another approach is the construction of a consistent range of costumes faithful to the subject matter and precise characters of the play. All these approaches have been used, adapted and combined, and have fed into ideas of modern costume design in the theatre.

Costume-design and -making

The procedure of dressing- and making-up and putting on a mask or headdress is often complicated. Not only may people be required to design and make the costumes, but often assistance is needed actually to make ready for the performance. There are a number of subsidiary functions to be carried out, though in a small company the tasks might be spread around:

Costume designer (the actor may perform this function, either choosing from stock or procuring what he/she needs);

Costumier, who makes or *builds* the costumes;
Wardrobe mistress (though it could be a man, of course), who looks after
the costumes in the theatre;
Dressers, who help the actors get ready.

In a production with complicated costumes and personal
props, there might be many more specialised staff, such as
mask-maker, wigmaker, armourer, bootmaker – in ballet
companies you need someone to look after the dancing
shoes – plus assistants. The complexity and available funds
will usually decide, except in the case of the costume designer
and the mask-maker, where changing conventions have
influenced the various responsibilities. In the *Noh* theatre, the
actor chooses his own costume, showing subtle interpretative
nuances of his roles through selection of colours and patterns.
The Renaissance in Europe, with its emphasis on a consistent
overall picture, first introduced the costume designer, who
conceptualised all the costumes for one production. The first

African 'medicine man' and English 'performer'

great costume designer in England, Inigo Jones, designed both scenery and costumes for the lavish Italianate masques presented at James I's court; it was not until much later, in the nineteenth and twentieth centuries, that commercial theatre managements habitually went to the expense of having costumes specially designed for each production. In primitive theatre, such as is found in Africa, America and in numerous folk festivals which survive in Europe and elsewhere, masks and costumes often remain unchanged for many generations.

Returning briefly to the primitive theatre, we may note that in many traditions widely separated in space and time, masks and disguise are sometimes so complete as to conceal the performers almost entirely.

This complete disguise is not unlike a form of theatre where the actors are present but not visible at all – the puppet theatre. Here may be the appropriate place to consider this specialised form of theatre.

Puppets and models

The heaviest disguise an actor can adopt is to manipulate, or speak through, a puppet. The puppeteer may not consider him/herself an actor at all, but a puppet is, in a sense, an extension of mask and costume, where the impersonation of character is so complete that the actor can remain separate from it. A puppet-maker is actually more like a sculptor than an actor. The story of Giacometto and his puppet Pinocchio, who came to life, was similar to that of Pygmalion, in Greek legend, who carved a statue which came to life. But the function of a puppet, unlike that of a statue, is to be heard to speak and seen to move, so although there is no human presence inside the puppet, one or more people are physically connected with it, by string, or rod, or hand.

Puppetry has been widespread through the world and through all ages. Sometimes, in countries where drama was disapproved of, it has been the only form of theatre. For example, there is evidence of puppet shows in many parts of the Islamic world, even though theatre was not allowed. One of the most famous puppet characters is Karagoz, a Turkish shadow puppet rather like the British Punch. Karagoz was an obscene, comic villain, who indulged in much sex and violence, to the hilarity of his audience. For centuries, and until quite recently, shows were performed in popular venues such as markets, coffee-houses and bathhouses. Somehow, puppets escaped official censure, because of their popular appeal and comic style, and because the performer was not physically disguising his/her own body. Turkey, placed geographically between Asia and Europe, was influenced by the popularity of shadow puppetry in many parts of the Islamic world. Through Mediterranean trade links, especially with Venice, Turkish theatre influenced the European, encouraging the development of such characters as Pulcinella in Italy, Polichinelle in France, Kasperl in Germany and Punch in Britain, all of whom bear some resemblance to Karagoz. Nowadays, radio and television comedy have taken over from the Turkish puppet shows, but, like Punch, the figure of Karagoz still features in modern comic satire as the name and logo of a magazine. The universality of such a figure is shown by the existence of a counterpart even in

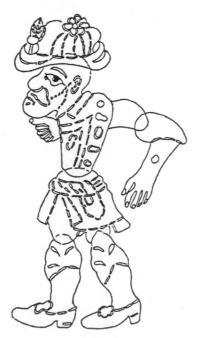

Karagoz, the Turkish puppet

eighth century China, where a jolly, rotund marionette figure known as Baldy Guo was popular during the Tan dynasty.

Shadow puppets are two-dimensional figures shown as silhouettes against a lighted screen. Popular in the Arab world and also in South East Asia, the most sophisticated versions are in Java. Here, intricate leather cut-out figures are mounted on sticks of buffalo horn. A complete set consists of up to 350 figures. A traditional performance lasts from evening to dawn, divided into periods which reflect the different stages of life. The Javanese shadow play is a religious and educational experience, teaching the audience about good and evil, according to its culture, influenced by Hinduism and Buddhism before it became Islamic. The audience sits on both sides of the screen, and the play is accompanied by an orchestra and singers.

In Japan, alongside the *Noh* and *Kabuki* theatre, developed *Bunraku* doll puppets, marionettes which grew to such manipulative complexity that each puppet had three operators. In Europe, both string marionettes and hand puppets were used by itinerant puppet-showmen, and at various times the art became a fashionable form of entertainment. Perhaps more significant than its sophisticated forms, has been the performing of dangerous or forbidden dramatic material through popular puppetry. In England, biblical puppet plays were performed centuries after religious drama had been banned, and in France and Italy, puppet shows in the nineteenth century were often the medium for political and social satire. This demonstrates the fact that distance or disguise removes the performers' personal responsibility for his/her material, allowing great licence to be taken. In Britain, satire has been created through the use of exaggerated, distorted puppet-figures in a television series called *Spitting Image*.

The technology of puppetry is often a source of enjoyable wonder for the spectator. The puppeteer is regarded as a kind of magician or conjuror, and just as with magical and conjuring tricks, the audience's reaction is finely balanced between admiration of human skill, and half-belief that it is not skill, but real magic.

Approaches to mask, costume and puppetry

Thus, mask, costume and puppet can be used to inform the audience that the actor is not himself, his whole self and nothing but himself. They can be used to project, to enhance, or to change his/her character. Western tradition gradually developed towards a realistic appearance, in which the actor imitated, as closely as possible, the period, place, age, rank, profession, social and physical type, and other circumstances of the role he adopted; while Eastern tradition developed styles which often aimed to transcend these circumstances, giving visual expression to the more universal and spiritual character traits. Throughout the world, comic, grotesque and satirical portrayals of mankind have been shown through exaggerated masks and puppets, allowing much freedom of expression through clownish roles. In many cultures, women have been presented by men because actresses were forbidden in plays, either by law or by custom. In primitive cultures, the mask, costumes and puppets themselves may be considered to have some intrinsic powers, providing a link between the world of living men, the natural environment and the world of gods, demons and spirits.

In the twentieth century, the European convention of realism has dominated the development of theatre in many parts of the world, but gradually the more exaggerated forms of disguise have come to be appreciated in the West too, for the power they exert on the audience. Huge models dominate much popular street theatre, such as the Thanksgiving parade in New York, as well as the experimental Bread and Puppet Theatre in San Francisco.

Whatever kind of disguise the actor uses, it always makes some statement to the audience about his or her presence. Often, in low-budget theatre productions, the designer looks for a cheap basic costume, such as putting the actors into leotards and tights, or dressing them in their ordinary clothes, with minor additions or modifications, such as hats. This is not to do *without* costumes, but to establish a simple costume convention acceptable to the audience. There is no such thing as *no* costume. Even nudity in the theatre is a kind of costume, and indeed a very controversial kind. Every kind of disguise, whether mask, make-up, robe or puppet, helps to establish the most basic theatrical convention which says: 'I am here, but not as myself alone'.

5

The art of acting

WE now come to the heart of the theatre, the art of acting, and we are immediately confronted with the central problem in reading or writing about the theatre. It is a fact that a theatrical performance is an event in time and does not exist afterwards. We know of it only through memory, hearsay or, in the last hundred years, through recordings, films or videos. The theatre building may exist, or it may have been demolished, or have changed to other uses; masks, costumes and props may survive, or only descriptions or pictures of them; playscripts may be studied, but little remains of dramatic ritual or of improvised drama. But before audio-visual technology could reproduce them, the actors' speech and movement were entirely lost, as Shakespeare was poignantly aware, when he wrote of:

> a poor player,
> That struts and frets his hour upon the stage
> And then is heard no more.
> *(Macbeth*, Act v, Scene v, l. 24)

Nevertheless, although individual performances live on only by reputation, we can trace in outline the main features of the actor's trade, and note its variations to suit audience expectations in different times and places. The actor's speech and movement together make up the content of drama; this chapter also begins to consider plays themselves, because they provide the framework for the actor's art.

'The actors are come hither'

Having noted the importance of the actor's living presence before his/her audience, we can see that the most basic requirement is that each actor *be* there, for the duration of his/her part in the play. This means that each one must arrive and depart. Obvious as this statement may appear, it opens up many features and variations in the actor's task.

We have seen two ways in which actors signal their arrival. One is by entering the space which has already been designated as the stage, whether it is an empty circle or an elaborately adorned proscenium stage. The other way is by putting on a mask or costume. There is a clear difference between theatrical conventions where actors are visible before the play begins, and conventions where they appear already in character. In many traditions there is some kind of prologue or preview, such as a procession round the village or town, as for the City Dionysia and the Corpus Christi plays, or an introductory announcement by a representative actor as happens in Chinese classical theatre. This preparation serves an advertising function, much as modern film previews or press interviews with star actors. But there are other traditions where the actors prepare themselves in privacy. Much ritual and folk drama gains its initial impact from the entrance into the public space, or the arrival at the door, of apparent strangers, like the Vagabonds mentioned in Chapter 2. Surviving rituals, like the apparent surprise and secrecy of Santa Claus's descent down the chimney, or the arrival of 'witches' and 'sprites' at Hallowe'en, remind us of the special excitement to be enjoyed in the odd mixture of knowing, and yet pretending *not* to know, that such beings are not really strangers.

In looking at stage spaces, we saw that most are designed with a curtain or other form of concealment. The words 'to make an entrance' show us that the actor's arrival on stage in character is a special moment, to be relished by audience and performers. In *Kabuki* theatre, particularly, the *hanamichi*, or flower way, provides a lengthy and impressive entrance.

Next, we must consider *who* enters, and *where* he/she stands. It may seem that these questions are too broad to answer, but a brief examination of two strict theatre forms, Greek tragedy and the Japanese *Noh*, will reveal some clear conventions which have been used.

In its earliest form, Greek tragedy consisted of a chorus and one character, the protagonist. The chorus, probably consisting of up to fifty people, performed in the orchestra, the circular space in front of the stage, sometimes beginning the play, and often remaining on stage throughout, commenting on the action and forming a link with the audience. They acted as a kind of group story-teller, but usually had a function within the story, perhaps as citizens of the town in which the story happened. The protagonist appeared on the raised stage, interacted with the chorus, and made exits and re-entrances as the story developed. Often the chorus-leader took a major part, as a kind of counsellor to the protagonist. As the dramatising of stories became more complicated, the antagonist was added, the person with whom the protagonist was in conflict. This meant that far more of the tension of the story was presented on stage. In later Greek tragedies, minor characters appeared, including the messenger, who described events taking place off-stage. Apart from the dancing, through which the chorus expressed the lyrical parts of the drama, Greek tragedy was probably performed rather statically, with a few select visual changes, such as the horrific last entrance of Oedipus the King in Sophocles' play of that name. Oedipus, having discovered he was the unknowing perpetrator of dreadful crimes he had been investigating, tore out his eyes off-stage, and entered with the empty sockets streaming with blood. His last exit was with his daughters, going into self-imposed exile, leaving the chorus to a final utterance of lamentation.

In the equally simple form of Japanese *Noh*, there is also a main character, the *shite*. His entrance is usually preceded by the *waki*, the person at the side, whose role, often as itinerant monk or priest, is to represent the audience, often asking questions and having little character of his own. Since *Noh* plays were not based on stories of conflict, no second character, equivalent to the antagonist, developed, but the *shite* might have one or more *isure*, or companion. There are also sometimes children's parts, as well as rustics and menials.

Before any of the characters in *Noh* appear, the musicians, chorus and understudies take their assigned places. The musicians are placed in prescribed order round the stage, the understudies behind and the chorus, who have no dramatic role, sit at the side and recite for the actors, particularly when they are dancing. All remain on stage throughout, within full view of the audience. The drama, often split into two scenes, is presented in a mixture of dance, speech and song. Several plays are presented in one programme, gradually increasing in intensity and excitement.

These two conventions show how the main concentration in serious drama has been on *one* character, the actor drawing the audience in to contemplate his/her experience intensively, and to consider its significance to themselves. The circumstances are filled out through supporting characters and a chorus, that is, an actor or group of actors who extend the expression of the drama without fully impersonating a character in the story. Many other plays can be seen to use actors and characters similarly, combining and varying these different kinds of actor-presence. For example, French tragedies of the seventeenth century adopted the classical Greek form, with its concentration on static drama, but dropped the group chorus. Instead, there was often a *confidant(e)*, a character to whom the protagonist poured out his/her troubles. Shakespearean drama also dropped the impersonal chorus figure, except as a prologue or epilogue to scenes, and used the soliloquy, direct speech by one character to the audience, to convey the protagonist's inner thoughts and feelings. Shakespeare's Hamlet is entirely alone on stage at some of the most highly charged moments in the play, confiding in the audience.

Another important convention showing the inner mental state of the main character was the medieval convention of allegory, where several actors portrayed *one* character, by representing different qualities. In *Everyman*, the main character met, one by one, different external characters and forces in his life. Later, the characters he encountered were parts of his own nature, such as Beauty, Strength, Five Wits, Discretion.

In all these conventions, the actor was present to show directly, or indirectly, the main character's state of mind and spirit. His/her entrances and exits within the action of the play were controlled by the story-telling factor, that is, the best order in which to convey to the audience what happened. For example, the story of Oedipus the King was not shown in the order in which events happened to Oedipus, but in the order in which he discovered their significance. Let us look now at a type of theatre where the events were shown more strictly in the order in which they might have happened, the popular comedy.

Stage events in comedy

From Roman comedies of the third century BCE, and probably long before, to farces performed in the West End of London today, laughter has often been based on entrances and exits. Who enters? When? Who sees them? Why do they exit? Why do they misunderstand the situation?

Here is an example from the second Act of *La Puce à l'Oreille* (*A Flea in her Ear*), a French farce written in 1907 by Georges Feydeau. You will not find it easy to understand in words, but if you work through this explanation with actors on a stage, or with a diagram of entrances, exits and labelled characters, you will follow the plot more clearly. The scene took place at the Hôtel Coq d'Or. The main characters were as follows:

Mme Chandebise – came to the hotel to unmask her husband's supposed unfaithfulness, having lured him there by a false assignation note written by her friend Lucienne.

Lucienne Homenides de Histangue – came to witness the unmasking of M. Chandebise.

Homenides de Histangue – came to catch his wife Lucienne red-handed with her supposed lover, and kill her, having recognised her handwriting in the assignation letter.

M. Chandebise – came to save Lucienne from her husband's wrath.

Complications arose around the identity of M. Chandebise because of the following characters:

M. Camille Chandebise (M. Chandebise's nephew) – came to keep an assignation with M. Chandebise's cook.

M. Tournel – came to take M. Chandebise's place at the supposed assignation.

Poche – present as the hotel porter – was coincidentally a

double of M. Chandebise (and was played by the same actor).

Many other complications were added, including:

Feraillon, the hotel manager – mistook M. Chandebise for Poche, dressed him in Poche's uniform, leaving Poche no option but to put on M. Chandebise's clothes.

Baptistin – was employed by Feraillon to pose as a rheumatic invalid, lying in a bed which, at the press of a button, revolved into the bedroom booked for M. Chandebise's assignation.

Herr Schwarz – occupied the nearby bedroom and wanted to make it with any woman who entered.

Etienne, M. Chandebise's butler, married to his cook – came with a message.

This was a different use of the actor's presence from the tragic and contemplative forms described earlier. Here, a story was acted out at the same rate it would be in life, except for some greater speed to increase the comic effect. The actors actually *did* what the people in the story did. This is what one of the first dramatic theorists, Aristotle, meant when he said that 'drama is an imitation of an action'. He was making a distinction between drama and narrative. When a story is narrated, the action is speeded up or slowed down; some episodes are skipped altogether, others elaborated, according to the emphasis the story-teller wants. But in comic farce, the moments are linked together in an unbreakable chain. The focus is not on *one* person's life, but on the connection between different people's entrances, actions and exits. Every moment, on or off the stage, has to be accounted for.

Acting is therefore based on two different uses of the actor's presence. One is an extension of the story-teller's art, where entrances and exits do not necessarily correspond with the time involved in the real-life events, where there has been some extension and reduction, as in story-telling, in order to highlight the most decisive, dramatic moments. The other is imitation of action, a pretence that the events on stage are actually happening. Here, examples of the first have been taken from serious drama, and an example of the second from comedy; but the art of acting has developed with a mixture of these conventions, in varying proportions, in many different kinds of plays.

Position on stage

The actor's instrument is his/her body. Once on stage he/she is moving or still, speaking or silent. The actor's skill therefore consists in making those states fully expressive to the audience. In the live theatre, only an exit removes the actor from the drama, while on the screen, the actor is often in the scene, but not in camera shot. On the stage, the transition from one state to another is an impressive part of the art. In both serious and comic drama, recognition is very important. Whether it is Oedipus recognising his own guilt, or the characters in *A Flea in her Ear* recognising Poche, whom they

The actor downstage

believe to be M. Chandebise, the changes from one state of awareness to another have to be conveyed to the audience.

Position on the stage is based on three spatial relationships. The first is with relation to the audience. The strongest position on stage is in the centre, from left to right, at an angle that allows the actor to see and be seen by the whole audience. The actor Laurence Olivier recommended 120° as the maximum angle between the actor and the audience at the extreme edges of the auditorium. Further towards the audience, downstage, makes for greater intimacy with the audience; further away, upstage, may increase dignity for the actor, and so will raising the actor up on a level. One of the most impressive entrances an actor can make is down a huge flight of stairs centre stage, the preferred star entrance in many spectacular entertainments. However strong the needs of realism, the position of the actors must always take into account the spatial relationship with the audience. In European theatre, even when realistic scenery was being introduced, it was for many years still customary for the actors to stand in a semi-circle, half-facing the audience. Still today, especially in opera and musicals, actors may break away from a realistic position, to take up a stronger relationship with the audience. And it has always been considered bad manners to upstage another actor, that is, to force him/her to take a weaker position on stage.

The second relationship which defines the actor's position is to the scenic elements. In the comedy we examined, the stage had to be arranged logically, and the actors' positions had to relate to that arrangement; but in much of Eastern theatre, there is little or no scenery to indicate location; and Greek tragedy took the location into account only minimally. In *Oedipus the King*, the stage area represented the palace doorway, making plausible the presence of Oedipus and the other characters, and the chorus. The more realistic the stage setting, the more the actor's position is dictated by its logic (see also Chapter 7).

The third spatial relationship is with other characters. Grouping is in itself expressive. For example, a character in one corner of the stage, while several others are grouped together, may indicate isolation, or even a conspiracy. Shakespeare was very skilled at placing characters on the stage expressively. He placed Juliet above Romeo in the scene where they declared love for each other; he isolated Hamlet from the rest of the royal court to express his disillusionment with the King and Queen; he made Macbeth half-avoid Lady Macbeth after killing their king, so that at first she did not see that he had brought the blood-stained daggers with him.

Change of position, that is a move, is equally important. It will often imply a change of status. For example, in *Richard II*, Shakespeare placed the king high on a balcony in the scene when he was deposed. When Richard saw his power gone, he came down on to the stage level, which represented the lower court of the castle, losing his dominating position. Walking from one position to another, the actor has to take the shape and size of the stage into account, moving rapidly or slowly, inconspicuously or obviously. In the *Noh* theatre, the stage is quite small, about eighteen foot square, while in Shakespeare's Globe it was over forty feet wide. In the first, it is important to make every tiny move carry its full impact, while in the second, the actor had to be able to cover space

Stage positions tell a story

quickly, keeping up the pace of the action, and creating interest for the audience.

Gesture

The language of gesture, often called body language now, is so eloquent that it has an art form of its own, the art of mime, pantomime or silent acting, where no words are used, and often no props or scenery. The imitation of bodily movement is a skill practised by dancers and actors throughout history. It may be part of a ritual, part of a story, part of a clowning act, part of a play, or a piece of entertainment in its own right. The power of mime is very great, because it is magical in its effect, creating a reality where there was none, getting to the heart of what theatre is. For this reason, it is hard to define or recapture. While the mime is going on, the audience is enthralled, convinced. Only when it is over do they remember to admire and observe what was done, whether it was a *commedia* actor trying to kiss the moon in a pond, a Chinese actor unbolting an imaginary door to enter an imaginary room, the French mime Marcel Marceau, showing the agony of a man who has a grinning mask stuck on his face, or the Victorian actor Henry Irving, reminded, by the sound of bells, of a crime he once committed:

> He moves his head slowly from us – the eyes still somehow with us – and moves it to the right – taking as long as a long journey to discover

The power of mime

the truth takes. He looks to the faces on the right – nothing. Slowly the
head revolves back again, down, and along the tunnels of thought and
sorrow, and at the end the face and eyes are bent upon those to the left
of him ... utter stillness ... nothing there either – everyone is
concerned with his or her little things – smoking or knitting or
unravelling wool or scraping a plate slowly and silently. A long pause,
endless, breaking our hearts, comes down over everything, and on and
on go those bells.
(The designer Gordon Craig, describing Henry Irving as Mathias in
The Bells which he first played in 1871.)

Conventions of stage gestures have varied as much as
conventions of stage costumes. There is the important
question of how realistic gestures on stage should be. In
general, the more decorative and symbolic the use of costume,
the more ritualised and dance-like becomes the use of gesture.
Thus, Indian theatre developed a complex language of
symbolic gestures, using prescribed movements of the head,
cheek, nose, eyebrows, neck, chin, chest, eyes, feet and hands,
while European realism led to the use of meticulously
naturalistic gestures, described in nineteenth-century England
as cup-and-saucer acting, and in the 1920s as flick of the
wrist acting.

Although a very skilful actor may make his tiny toe
expressive, the most expressive part of the body is the face,
especially the eyes, and the mouth. Where a mask is worn,
the facial expression depends on the skilful use of the mask.
When the eyes are visible, a more personal relationship can
be developed between actor and actor, and between actor
and audience.

Just as expressive, in a different way, are hands, which can
develop their own sign language. Sign language is partly
imitative, and partly conventional, with no direct connection
between the sign and the meaning. The art of mime, too,
occasionally resorts to conventional language; for example, a
hand circling the fact indicates beauty; rolling the hands over
one another above the head, is an invitation to dance.

In ordinary life, there is great variety in the meaning of
gestures, gestures which have developed, both naturally and
artificially, in different parts of the world at different times.
From military ceremonial – for example, various forms of
salute – to different ways of being vulgar, cultures develop

their own vocabulary, which the actor can observe, and use whenever appropriate. The history of gesture is largely unrecorded. In Shakespeare's time, books of rhetoric were published, showing persuasive gestures, but such books do not make it any easier to understand what is meant, for example, when a servant in *Romeo and Juliet* bites his thumb to show insolence. Shakespeare's audience might be equally mystified by the modern British nudge, nudge, wink, wink.

Voice

The final piece of the actor's expressive equipment would be considered by many people the most important – the voice, through which men and women share their passions, thoughts, intentions and reflections.

Vocal skill has been universally cultivated and recognised in everyday life as well as in the theatre. It might be a hunter's imitation of birds and animals; the soothing sound of an old nanny nursing a child to sleep; the reading of a beautiful piece of poetry; or the comic mimicry of an actor like Peter Ustinov, who can imitate the sound of a tractor, or of a conversation held in a neighbouring room. In theatre, the vocal skills required have depended on the size of the space, as well as on changes in convention, and range of opportunity within that convention. The first essential is that the actor must be as clearly audible as he/she is visible, whether the theatre is large or small, outdoors or indoors, purpose-built or hastily adapted for a play.

Actors in Shakespeare's time had to be particularly adaptable. They performed in the partially open-air Globe, which seated 3000 people, as well as in the more intimate indoor Blackfriars theatre and at Court. When touring, they had to adapt again, adjusting voice and movement to the size and shape of whatever theatre they performed in. Many other traditions have been more fixed, allowing the actor to specialise in the vocal skill required by just one kind of theatre, such as the Japanese *Noh*, the Restoration apron stage, or the large theatres of the late eighteenth and nineteenth centuries.

Consider this question: which is the greater vocal skill, to set the rafters ringing with a grand rhetorical display that stretches the lungs and resonators of the human voice? Or to let the tiniest whisper reach the most distant member of the audience, drawing him into an illusion of intimacy with the actor? Both skills are part of the artistic equipment of a versatile actor.

In Greek theatre, the mask acted as an amplifier, which the actor had to use with skill, learning not to distort the sound, as a musician must learn how to use his instrument, and how to create the purest expression of the language. In modern theatre, the voice can be amplified by electronic means. Just as a mask has the power to concentrate facial expression, and so does the film or television screen, similarly, the microphone focuses and exaggerates the voice. Many actors trained in the live theatre, especially in large buildings, lament the vocal weakness of their younger colleagues, trained in small theatres and in recording studios. But microphone technique is also a skill. The actor has to learn, like the Japanese mask-less actor, to do *less*, so as not to compete with the microphone's effect. Modern actors, often unable to predict the field of acting they will enter, now have to be prepared to be as vocally adaptable as Shakespeare's actors, moving from television studio to live theatre perhaps within the same day.

The most expressive vocal tool is speech. And no one has surpassed Shakespeare in exploiting the power of speech in the theatre. It is therefore worth giving some attention to his achievement.

Speech in Shakespeare's theatre

Where the mime artist uses gesture to create reality and dreams out of nothing, Shakespeare gave his actors the opportunity to do it with words. The Chorus in *Henry V* suggests to his audience:

> Think, when we talk of horses, that you see them,
> Printing their proud hooves in the receiving earth.
>
> (Act I, Scene i, l. 26)

In Shakespeare's time, new ideas of all kinds, political, philosophical and geographical, were bursting forth. The printing press was a century old but still only a minority of the population could read. The spoken word was the perfect medium to express the alertness of mind, the wealth of opportunity, the ruthlessness and the wonder of the times. And Shakespeare combined this with his own kind of mimicry, an ear to hear the language of the common people as well as of the princes, and an ability to paint vivid word pictures. Remembering the different kinds of functions actors have on the stage, let us examine how Shakespeare divided and combined the functions of the story-teller, the protagonist and the acting-out of events in front of the audience.

In Shakespeare's plays, the story-telling was shared between the characters. Battle scenes were often reported by a swift sequence of messengers, adding to the tension of the scene. The messenger role might also be a lyrical one. For example, in *Hamlet* the Queen relates the pathetic death of Ophelia, who loved Hamlet, in a speech of vivid poetic narrative:

> There is a willow grows aslant the brook
> That shows his hoar leaves in the glassy stream;
> There with fantastic garlands did she come
> Of crowflowers, nettles, daisies, and long purples
> (Act iv, Scene vii, l. 166)

Shakespeare showed masterly and very individual judgment in deciding what was to be told to the audience through messenger characters, and what was to be enacted before their eyes. Greek tragedians, Japanese *Noh* playwrights and comedy writers often obeyed established conventions; but Shakespeare manipulated language and action in innovative ways. One feature of his writing was that, although much depended on the spoken word, there were moments when, as in mime, the visual action contained the full meaning. For example, in one of his last plays, *The Winter's Tale*, a statue comes slowly and breathtakingly alive, and in *King Lear*, the old, blinded Duke of Gloucester believes he is standing on top of a cliff and takes a suicidal leap, which simply lands him on the level ground in front. Both these dramatic moments are purely visual.

Another important aspect of Shakespeare's writing was his treatment of the protagonist. To explore the protagonist's situation more deeply, Shakespeare presented characters who were parallel, or in contrast, to the main character. For example, the Duke of Gloucester, mentioned above, went through some of the same experiences as King Lear himself. By considering *both* men's plight, the audience was able to understand the central experience more fully. Shakespeare's method of working created a huge variety and richness of parts for actors. It was similar to music of the same period: Renaissance music was exploring polyphony, meaning 'many sounds', with several voices blending and clashing together. In the same way, in Shakespeare's texts, *many* characters carried the events of the story in words and actions. And in any one play, several characters might suffer an experience of some depth, though the experience of one or two still remained central.

Shakespeare also lifted the story-telling aspect of drama to new heights. He exploited every rhetorical device to convey the circumstances and the significance of events – imagery, rhythm and metre, word-play, and a vast and eloquent vocabulary – all harnessed in the pursuit of the drama. Often, at moments of great dramatic impact for the character – for example, when King Lear goes mad in the middle of a storm, and when Juliet takes a potion that will make her appear dead – Shakespeare imposed on the actor the full burden of conveying the atmosphere and significance of what was happening.

Comparison with voice in Afro/Asian theatre

The voices of Shakespeare's actors had to be capable of a great range of expression, every nuance made clear, in a large, open theatre with many distractions. Voice in African and Asian theatre developed along a different tradition from the European. The physical and emotional potential of the human voice remains the same in any culture, but the more self-contained cultures outside Europe did not develop the emphasis on persuasion of Western man. From the Greek study of oratory, the Romans and the Catholic Church learnt to use language to spread intellectual and social ideas in politics, religion and the theatre. The use of the voice was closely linked with the framing of sentences, sermons and public speeches. The connection between one thought and another had to be clear. Pauses, emphases and inflections (the rise and fall of the voice), all had to be calculated, by training or natural skill, so as to convey the accumulating meaning of what was being said. Elsewhere that discursive flow was less important. The sound of the African and Asian languages sometimes strikes the European ear as unmelodious. In drama, the disjointed effect is often greater. The actor bypasses the logic of language to explore pure utterance – the power of incantation, the expression of extreme emotion, the limits of physical experience, the communication of his/her innermost self and spirituality. When, towards the end of the nineteenth century, Europeans first encountered Eastern theatre, the effect was often shattering. The French writer, Antonin Artaud, for example, was immensely excited by his experience of Balinese theatre in Paris, in 1931:

> What is in fact curious about all these gestures, these angular and abruptly abandoned attitudes, these syncopated modulations formed at the back of the throat, these musical phrases that break off short, these flights of elytra, these rustlings of branches, these dances of animated manikins, is this: that through the labyrinth of their gestures, attitudes and sudden cries, through the gyrations and turns which leave no portion of the stage space unutilized, the sense of a new physical language, based upon signs and no longer upon words, is liberated.
> (From *The Theater and its Double*, by Antonin Artaud, Grove Press, New York, 1958)

The intensity of Artaud's reaction may have been partly because he did not understand the language. (Just as the acting in a foreign language film can sometimes seem to us more powerful because we do not understand the words.) But Artaud did point out an important difference: the Balinese performers were free of the constraints of reasonableness which were dominating European theatre of the time, based on its confidence in the power of rational speech. This dominance was in the legitimate theatre, the respectable, classical theatre tradition which had first developed in the court and city theatres, a tradition hallowed by the development, from the Renaissance onwards, of academic criticism. One way of understanding what the art of theatre has come to mean in various cultures, is to examine the methods of actor training.

The training of an actor

In India, China, Japan and South East Asia, the art of theatre was always associated with strict codes of behaviour and discipline. The Hindu temple was the training-ground for Sanskrit theatre; Confucianism formed the basis of the social system in China, out of which theatre grew; Buddhist practice and philosophy, and also military discipline, influenced the development of the sophisticated Japanese forms of theatre; while in other parts of Asia, such as Thailand, Burma, Cambodia, Java and Bali, the Eastern religions all had their effect on philosophy and customs. In each of these countries it was recognised that actors and dancers must be trained. That training has been an arduous technical process, rather like training for classical ballet or opera.

In India, the training of female temple dancers began very early in its history. The study of Indian classical dance is still a long, difficult process. While the acting of plays may not require quite so much discipline, the dominance of the dance form still makes rigorous training necessary. In China, acting academies existed as early as the eighth century, when the Emperor Xuanzong funded the conservatory of the Pear Orchard. To be 'a member of the Pear Orchard' meant – to be an actor.

In Europe, the Catholic Church was ambivalent about the theatre. At first acting was condemned as forcefully as in Moslem countries, but in the Middle Ages, the Church itself brought about a flowering of the drama, and later, the cultural developments of the Renaissance brought a recognition that the arts were important in their own right. Nevertheless, there was little formal training until the twentieth century. Most actors learned their craft through being apprenticed in the theatre. Often family traditions grew up, and still today the craft may be handed on from one generation to another, as with circus and variety entertainers. In schools, only one subject related directly to acting and that was the art of rhetoric, which was a regular part of a classical education in Europe, influenced by the schools in Ancient Greece.

In Africa, as in other countries where rural theatre has

thrived, acting as a separate profession was slow to develop. Training for ritual drama was integrated into the whole educational process, while the skill of the story-teller was handed on through individual teaching. Dancing, too, was taught as part of the general education of the young in many tribes.

Three methods of training have emerged, then, and we can see each being dominant in particular periods and places. The most sophisticated kind of training is provided in conservatories and academies dedicated to the development of performers skilled in a particular discipline. Students are taught in an enclosed environment, perhaps separated from their families from an early age. This kind of training occurs when the art of acting is recognised as a specialised activity in the community. The second method is apprenticeship, when skills are taught on the job by those already trained, and the trainee progresses gradually from the lowest rungs of the profession. This method is so commonplace that it often goes unrecorded, but we can surmise that throughout the world, wherever entertainment has been needed and provided, performers have banded together to cultivate their skills in acting, singing, dancing, story-telling, juggling and acrobatics. Craft guilds and companies have been formed. Sometimes, when such companies disintegrate (as happened in parts of Europe at the end of the nineteenth century), or when the art is raised to an elite position in society (as happened with *Noh* theatre in Japan), formal schools have replaced this more casual method of training.

The third method occurs when acting and related skills are built into general education. Speech and elocution have often been taught in private schools in Europe, while drama is now part of the curriculum in many public and private schools in the West. But integrated drama is not a new subject. It is actually as old as the earliest forms of theatre, in which members of a community learnt the rituals believed necessary to their welfare.

Each method of training shows the status of acting within a society. With the dominance of Western culture, many non-Western countries developed schools to teach European theatre techniques. Also, recognising that indigenous theatre traditions were being threatened, people formed schools where those traditions could be fostered and taught to new generations. In modern Africa, for example, universities such as Ibadan, in Nigeria, are centres for the cultivation and development of black theatre. Now, many would-be actors seek a training that will equip them to perform different kinds of theatre. Or else they seek a style of acting that unifies the various performance traditions. The International Company of Peter Brook, mentioned earlier, aspires to that kind of common acting style.

Acting skills are closely connected with associated skills such as dancing, singing, story-telling and so on. As we have seen, different traditions have emphasised different combinations of skills, with the European classical tradition specialising in rhetoric, while many Asian traditions specialise in dance/drama. All acting, however, involves impersonation, the taking on of another role. Yet even this skill, which is the very essence of the art of acting, has been widely interpreted. Let us consider three approaches to it.

Stanislavsky and the illusion of reality

One of the most dominant approaches to the art of acting reached its zenith at the end of the nineteenth century in Russia, when Konstantin Stanislavsky, one of the first eminent directors in the theatre, founded the Moscow Arts Theatre in 1896, and developed an acting system which he wrote about in several books. (*The Actor Prepares*, *Building a Character* and *Creating a Role* are the main ones.) His aim was to find ways in which an actor could create – and recreate – truth and freshness in a performance. But what kind of truth? For Stanislavsky, *truthful* acting was a faithful, authentic creation by the actor of the behaviour of the character he was playing. He believed that the achievement of theatre was to create the temporary illusion that what the audience saw and heard were real events. To this end, he devised many brilliant exercises which helped the actor to reject what was sham, and seek in his own imagination, observation, emotion and memory, until his experience and purpose matched the character's.

In this method, every detail of a performance has to fit the circumstances of the character. The actor therefore makes much effort to observe and express accurately, and to envisage the character as a complete person. While Stanislavsky was the greatest proponent of this method, it can also be seen as the shaping force behind every comment that praises *naturalness* in an actor, the sense that the actor is not putting on a special show, and also behind admiration for an actor's ability to convince us he/she *is* the character portrayed. The following lines are from an epitaph written about Shakespeare's leading actor, Richard Burbage, who died in 1619:

> Oft have I seen him leape into a grave
> Suiting ye person (which he seemed to have)
> Of a sad lover, with so true an eye
> That then I would have sworn he meant to die:
> So lively, ye spectators, and the rest
> Of his sad crew, while hee but seemed to bleed
> Amazed thought that he had died indeed. . . .
> How to ye person hee did suit his face,
> How did his speech become him, and his face
> Suit with his speech, whilst not a word did fall
> Without just weight to balance it withall.

These criteria for good acting have dominated the evolution of European acting. The modern actor Laurence Olivier was often praised for his brilliant impersonations, but dispraised because his craft was too apparent. It was assumed that what the actor was supposed to do was to create the illusion that the audience was watching the natural behaviour of a real person.

Acting as an art form

What we have so far observed about the actor in the *Noh* theatre has shown us that his approach to acting is a very different one. Here, the art is to distil a spiritual and emotional experience into voice and movement. Precise circumstances are irrelevant and must be transcended. In visual art, this kind of distillation is paralleled in expressionism, a term coined in the late nineteenth century in Europe to describe a form of painting which aimed to distort the reality we see on the surface, in order to express a truth beyond it. Another European art movement of the time called itself symbolist, and also paralleled Japanese art in seeking to bypass the details which make people and events different from each other, in order to reach what is shared between them. The Irish poet and playwright William Butler Yeats was inspired by his experience of Japanese *Noh* theatre to seek the same kind of clarity. He strove for simplicity and the eradication of anything that was extraneous to the inner truth:

> We must simplify acting. . . . We must get rid of everything that is restless, everything that draws attention away from the sound of the voice, or from the few moments of intense expression, whether that expression is through the voice or through the hands; we must from time to time substitute for the movements that the eye sees the nobler movements that the heart sees, the rhythmical movements that seem to flow up into the imagination from some deeper life than that of the individual soul.
>
> (From *Samhain* [September 1903], quoted in *Dramatic Theory and Criticism, Greeks to Grotowski* ed. Bernard F. Dukore, Holt, Rinehart & Winston, US, 1974)

The Greek theatre was another tradition that did not seek total realism, using masks and strict conventions to remind the audience and the actor that they were experiencing a highly artificial expression of human behaviour. When Europeans rediscovered the classical tradition in the sixteenth and seventeenth centuries, they took pride in imitating the dignity and artifice of Greek tragedy. Actors were required to declaim, to entone the verse. This was especially true of the French classical tradition of the seventeenth century, where, in the plays of Racine for example, the most searing passions were expressed in beautifully pointed language and formalised gestures, rather than in the frenzied behaviour the circumstances would have demanded in real life.

In the eighteenth century, much controversy raged about the accomplishments of individual actors in England, France and Italy. The declamatory style and the natural style were seen as two different schools of acting. The natural school paved the way for Stanislavsky's methods.

Another line of thought behind the belief in acting as an artificial form arose from the clear division, both in Eastern and Western theatre, between comedy and serious drama. Since the aim of comedy is usually to arouse laughter, every means must be found, through exaggeration, timing and the ability to point up what is happening, to make the audience see the funny side. In tragedy, on the other hand, the aim is to arouse tears. It is a paradox of acting that if the performer gets entirely involved with grief, he/she often fails to move the audience to experience it. There is disagreement over whether or not the actor must *feel* the appropriate emotion while expressing it. Tragedy and *Noh* drama must arouse a contemplative attitude in its audience. If the audience have too great a sense that what they are watching is part of the continuous stream of real events, then that contemplative attitude may not be achieved. The actor must bring the audience to a sense of the climax of the play, and then to its reflective conclusion.

Acting as play

The approaches outlined above demand a considerable array of skills, both imaginative and aesthetic. Together with training for the physical requirements already discussed, they amount to a discipline which forms the basis for many acting schools and training programmes. One approach, though, puts less emphasis on developing the actor's special powers. Instead, it emphasises the *pretence*, the knowledge shared by audience and actors that a play is being presented.

This approach was used in the Corpus Christi plays. In such a reverent period, it might be thought surprising that an ordinary citizen should shamelessly portray Christ, the Son of God. He did it by acknowledging that he was playing a game. The audience was not expected to believe in a fiction, but to share in the play as a reminder of the truth:

> You bakers, see that the same words you utter,
> As Christ hym self spake them, to be a memoriall
> Of that death and passion which *in play* ensue after shall.
> (From the Chester Banns)

Later, Shakespeare made fun of this approach in *A Midsummer Night's Dream*, making a timid fellow play the part of the lion and reassure the ladies in the audience that he was not really a lion:

Then know that I as Snug the joiner am
A lion fell, nor else no lion's dam
For if I should as lion come in strife
Into this place, 'twere pity on my life.

(Act v, Scene i, l. 226)

Yet Shakespeare too, exploited the *play* idea, by reminding the audience from time to time that they were in a theatre. Especially, he liked to compare life in the world with a play. The famous lines from *As You Like It* (All the world's a stage, and all the men and women merely players), link actors and audience in a shared awareness that what the actor was doing was the same as what we do in life – act out our role as best we can.

This approach to acting exploits the fact that the tools the actor uses are the same ones used in ordinary life – speech and gesture. The distinction between actor and audience can be blurred. It is an approach that works best in a theatre space where the separation between them is not unbridgeable. As the proscenium stage became popular in Europe, the actors cut themselves off from the audience and gave more attention to establishing the fiction on the stage, creating the illusion of reality which Stanislavsky would help to bring to its finest fruition.

Yet even as the Stanislavsky approach reached its peak, the *play* approach was being rediscovered. Several European playwrights took up the Shakespearean theme of exploring the parallels between life and theatre. One in particular, Bertolt Brecht, trained actors to strive for what he called *Verfremdungseffekt* ('alienation effect'). For this effect, an actor would make it clear that he/she was detached from the character, playing a part in order to demonstrate behaviour so that an audience could learn from it. And as the field of psychology opened up, new parallels emerged, as psychologists unveiled the psychodramas and the role-playing carried out in real life. And in education *playing* was discovered to be an effective way in which children learnt. The art of acting began to merge with the need to learn the art of living. Nowadays, a television documentary will sometimes show a slice of real life served up in exactly the same way as fiction, for our entertainment and enlightenment.

In search of truth

The final question to consider about acting is whether these approaches are mutually exclusive or merely a matter of changing emphasis. The Shakespearean theatre showed that all three approaches might be appropriate within one play. Shakespeare depicted characters of great physical and psychological depth, and only those actors who can convince us of their plausibility and spontaneity satisfy the audience. For example in one scene of *Hamlet* the hero sees the ghost of his own father. Actors through the centuries have been praised or condemned for how well they convinced the audience of genuine terror at that moment. Yet, a few scenes later, Hamlet is to be found commenting on his disgust with mankind, in a speech which ostentatiously reminds the audience that he is not in Denmark, but in a wooden theatre, strutting on a stage covered with a ceiling, on which stars and moons are painted to represent the heavens. And throughout the play, the part of Hamlet is written in blank verse requiring rhetorical expertise to deliver, and of such length and range that only an actor of enormous physical stamina can make it through to the last scene, let alone finish with a dexterous sword fight and final surge of poetry.

When the acting is inappropriate it fails to convince, as the rustic actors fail in *A Midsummer Night's Dream*. When smaller theatres became popular in Europe, and when the camera and microphone revealed the slightest flicker or nuance in a performance, then large-scale acting became out of place; actors were accused of being ham, the slang word for over-acting. Declamatory styles were rejected in favour of more naturalistic styles. Yet other audiences found naturalism unsatisfying because it was dull. They disliked it for being as confused and inaudible as people's real lives.

But if we think someone's acting is bad, because it fails to convince us, we have to ask the question: 'Fails to convince of *what?*' The root of theatre is a communal search for the truth which speech and gesture can reveal. The player acts, or the actor plays, for the sake of a truth which ordinary behaviour obscures. The audience is invited to look and to listen. Perhaps they will be swept up in a drama that makes them entirely forget their ordinary lives. The *magic* of theatre will transport them into a make-believe world, sad or funny or wonderful, which seems real for a while; just as a dream seems real until you wake. Has that dream world, on the other side of ordinary life, anything valuable and truthful to tell us or not? We must turn to philosophy or psychology to answer that question.

In some drama, the *truth* is considered so powerful that actors need only play at the action for it to be revealed. In performances with a powerful non-theatrical aim behind them, the actor's job is simply to channel the message through. Examples include: medieval Christian drama; tribal fertility rites performed in order to help crops grow and the earth replenish itself; anti-war plays aimed at making the audience change the way the world is going; psychodrama, where a patient may be on the edge of breakthrough to their personal truth.

When a skilled actor involves him/herself deeply in a role, he/she imitates suffering, both in comedy and tragedy, and distils that suffering into a pleasurable experience for the audience. Perhaps he/she is redeeming the audience from suffering, like a scapegoat, or a healer. The Greek philosopher Aristotle called this effect catharsis – a purging or cleansing of the emotions.

Whatever we understand the theatre to be, the essential task of the actor is to play a role. In the different social uses of theatre throughout the world, the actor has been cast, at various times, as priest, artist, entertainer, teacher, story-teller, magician or victim, as well as whatever character he/she portrays. His/her achievement as an actor has been measured according to those very different tasks.

6
The play

WHEN the time, the place and the people are all prepared, a *play* is performed. What the play might be is the subject of this chapter. A play is a story or event presented through actors, each of whom performs a different part in the whole. Plays demand the live participation of actors and audience, for a few hours at most. While it is possible to tell *any* story through drama, the conventions of theatre – live performance in real time and space – impose certain restrictions, and make some kinds of stories particularly dramatic. Let us begin with stories themselves.

Stories – fact or fiction

Each culture develops its own collection of stories dealing with the beliefs of the community. Over 40,000 years ago, mankind scattered about the globe. Beginning in Africa, men and women spread through Europe, Asia and Australia, and later to North and South America. By 20,000 years ago, physical evolution had more or less ended. The communities that were established by then were isolated from each other, and developed different stories and religions, but those stories answered the same basic questions, and they dealt with the same basic problems. These are myths. From Celts and Vikings in the northern hemisphere to Australian aborigines and New Zealand Maoris in the southern; from Incas in Peru to ancient Egyptians; the different groups created stories, characters, gods and goddesses, spirits good and evil, expressing their ideas of the natural and the supernatural, the human and the superhuman. To gather all these stories together would be a superhuman task, but you can research the myths of individual cultures, and see how they dealt with the same basic experiences in life.

As soon as men and women began to think, they wanted explanations about how they fitted into the cosmos, and into their own community. They invented stories about the creation of the world, and the creation of mankind, in order to pass on the explanation to their children. They invented stories about the people who came before them, and about the life-cycle. When agriculture began, people became aware of the eternal pattern of birth, growth and death which occurred in the yearly seasons, bringing the crops, a pattern which was paralleled in the cycles of human generations. Continuity could only be sustained through the community. Therefore, it was important to pass on wisdom from one generation to the next. Stories which explained creation, birth, growth, the passing on of wisdom, death and regeneration, sustained each culture.

Here is an example of a creation story, quoted in a modern play. It is attributed to the Xingu tribe in Brazil.

> *Origin of the stars.*
> The children were always hungry.
> Their parents said: 'We give you all we can, why do you complain?'
> But the children only cried and said again that they were hungry.
> In the ashes of the fire their mother found the jaw-bone of an ass and
>   threw it to them.
> They took what meat they could from the bone and divided it among
>   the youngest.
> When they saw there was nothing left, they knew that they would have
>   to leave.
> They joined hands, sang a song and climbed slowly up into the sky.
> Their mother said: 'Come back, come back. We will find more food for
>   you. Forgive us.'
> And the children answered: 'There is nothing to forgive.
>   We know you did what you could. We bear no grudge.'
> They said: 'We are better gone. Here we can help you.
>   Here we can help to lift the darkness from you.'
> And they became stars.
> (From *Savages* by Christopher Hampton, Faber and Faber, London,
> 1974)

From evidence of funeral rites, it is clear that human beings believed, from early days, that what happened to their mothers, fathers and forebears directly affected them. In Australia, for example, the aborigines are much preoccupied with the *dream time* – a period before living memory, when, they believe, their ancestors walked the earth. Many people have also believed in a close connection between human beings and nature. All over the world, myths arose in which human beings died and were reborn, just as plants and trees renew themselves. The telling of these stories was believed to contribute to the future welfare of the community. Examples include: the Greek myth of Demeter and Persephone; the Egyptian story of Isis and Osiris; an Indonesian story of a girl called Hainewele, who was murdered, and her body cut into pieces: where these pieces were buried, said the story, new varieties of plants grew which have fed human beings ever since.

Myths provide explanations for events beyond man's control. Often, in early myths, the explanation was supernatural. The characters were superhuman – gods and goddesses with powers greater than ordinary mortals. They were a kind of personification of external forces. For example, thunder was personified as Thor in Norse mythology, as Zeus in Greece. Early myths were often associated with religion because they were stories which explained the mysteries of human existence.

What has this to do with drama? Early myths linked with drama in two ways. First of all, they established the importance of the story-teller. In every culture the need to pass on stories has been important. In literate societies, stories can be passed on through the written word. But in non-literate societies the oral tradition is a great strength, giving people a sense of their own history and social identity. In Senegal, the story-teller is called the *griot*. He has been described as the chronicler of the people's history, and as the voice of the people's conscience. In nomadic societies, such as some North American Indians, and the desert Arabs, the story-teller helps to bind the community together. As people gather round the fire to hear his tales, a one-man piece of theatre is created. In scattered societies, the travelling story-teller serves the same function, as did the bards and minstrels of medieval Europe, performing their stories in castles and houses up and down the lands. The traditional story-teller is both a poet and a performer, and often a composer and singer as well.

Drama also connects with myth through ritual. Common

wisdom tells us that it is not enough to know: you must act on what you know. From earliest times, myths have been acted out as part of rituals to ensure the continuance of the community. Religious practices, social rules and taboos, and ritual drama are inextricably bound together through the enactment of myths.

Myths are based on what a community believes is true, but they may not be literally true. There will always be argument about the truth of the story of Adam and Eve, for example, but the myth will have life as long as its meaning still has truth for the community. Some of the Greek myths gained new significance with the development of Freudian psychology in the twentieth century. The story of Oedipus, for example, was seen in a new light when Sigmund Freud revealed the unconscious desire of the son for his mother.

The earliest societies explained life and death through the idea of ancestor-gods, demons and spirits. They saw themselves as intimately connected with the cycles of nature. The great religions of the world provided people with whole systems of beliefs, and suggested a special role for mankind within the system. Myths and legends then grew up around those central beliefs, and theatre was used to enact some of them. The drama of medieval Europe was built on the Christian stories, including the events of the bible and the lives of the saints; Sanskrit drama in India was based on two great cycles of Hindu myths, the *Mabharata* and the *Ramayana*, which spread to other parts of Asia as well. Greek myths inspired the great Athenian tragedies.

After stories of gods and spirits came legends and histories that delved into the known past of the community, strengthening its sense of community spirit and moral values. Each community found its own heroes, heroines and villains, whether they were David and Goliath, the Buddha, Saint Joan or Adolf Hitler.

Then there are fictional stories, tales with invented characters and situations. Fiction has a kind of truth, like myth. We are often told at the end of a film that the characters bear no resemblance to anyone living or dead, but this is not correct. If they were unlike people in real life, audiences would not believe in them. The statement is a safeguard, like the actor's mask and costume, protecting the

authors from actions for libel or slander, and reminding us
that the film-makers are not responsible for the characters'
actions. But, like characters in a myth, they represent a kind
of generalised or universal truth. For example, one of the
biggest collections of modern myths is the American Western,
with its recognisable hero, based on legend, and on a belief
in certain values in the community.

Thus, although myths and legends are often very old
stories, whose origins are lost in the mists of time, they are
similar to the most modern genres of fiction, in seeking to
make a pattern of human behaviour which is of some value
to the community, either by teaching them something or by
amusing them. Myths arise through the sharing of wisdom
and knowledge throughout a community. In old communities,
or those that have kept to old ways, the wisdom was held by
witch doctors, priests and elders of the community. Sometimes
it seems that that has all changed in modern society. But it
may be only the names that have changed. In many societies
philosophers and scientists have held the wisdom and
knowledge. They do not give names like Zeus or Aphrodite,
Christ or Satan, to the forces they discern; it is left to writers
and actors to personify the truths of modern culture. What
could be more mythical than the characters of Frankenstein
and his monster, invented by Mary Shelley to explain the
dangers of unbridled scientific exploration?

Myths have often dealt with the past, and with the forces
in the present which are outside man's control. But, seeking
to know their place in the cosmos, men and women have also
sought wisdom and knowledge about the future. Here, too,
the way to visualise the future has not altered as much as we
might think, from the oldest to the newest communities.
Dreams, prophecies and predictions, which were part of the
knowledge of ancient communities, are still shared in modern
societies. But, just as the discovery of evolution necessitated
new stories about man's creation and development, so new
fields of human affairs, such as economics and politics, have
produced new kinds of prophets in the guise of experts, who
are called upon to pronounce, warn, predict, even lay curses
on their community. ('If the Opposition gets in, it will spell
ruin for our country.') While dreams have been given a new
validity by psychology, they are rarely referred to nowadays

for foreknowledge about society as a whole. Instead, group fantasies take the form of science fiction, which often creates myths to explain the future.

So stories, which form the basis of drama, have their own kind of truth. They exist in the community as myths, legends, histories, or fiction. Stories often last much longer than seems reasonable. Even when the received wisdom has long been rejected as superstitution (belief in witches, for example), there is often some truth which still draws people to the tale, finding some satisfaction from their ancestors' way of explaining things.

Thus, through dramatic stories, people can deal with their deepest thoughts and their most serious preoccupations. But another aspect of drama presents simpler truths, by imitating human behaviour for popular amusement. In many cultures an alternative approach to theatre runs alongside the drama of established values, often turning it topsy turvy through laughter and ridicule. This popular form of drama is more difficult to trace through history, but is a no less important part of theatrical tradition.

Popular comedy and satire

While myths, legends and serious fiction deal with mankind's highest aspirations, popular comedy depicts the least divine and heroic of human characteristics. Its trademarks are vulgarity and ribaldry. From Etruscan comedies performed in Roman times, to modern television sitcoms, audiences have enjoyed recognising their weaknesses and foibles by seeing them exaggerated in dramatic form. The best-known comic types are those presented in the *commedia* troupes, but similar stereotypes can be found in other traditions, such as the *Kyogen* plays in Japan or the comedies of ancient Greece, as well as in screen entertainers such as Laurel and Hardy, the Marx Brothers, Charlie Chaplin and Buster Keaton.

In such plays, physical characteristics are important – such as being fat or skinny, ugly or old, in contrast with stereotypes of beauty and good looks. Stories are built around human weaknesses and vices – greed, stupidity, arrogance, vanity, lust, hypocrisy, cowardice and cruelty. Although these qualities are unpleasant, comedy makes them enjoyable.

In comic stories, the virtues of goodness, common sense and beauty sometimes triumph. People do not really believe, perhaps, that a villain can be put down or reformed in the time it takes to perform a comedy, but they enjoy a comforting, sometimes sentimental escape from the evils that beset human life.

Some comedies, such as satires, are not sentimental. Plays which exaggerate human vices can also be used as critical weapons against evils in society. For this reason, some drama has been suppressed by ruling authorities, because of the danger it poses to them. This raises the question of censorship in the theatre. But before considering that, there is another aspect of drama to be examined – its relation to conflict and violence.

Violence in the theatre

Greek tragedies did not present violence on the stage. Instead, violent deeds, such as that of Oedipus, who scratched out his own eyes and blinded himself, were narrated by a messenger, the effect transmuted through his reaction and that of his hearers. Yet the theatre of the Roman Empire presented spectacles of shocking violence and decadence, including gladiatorial displays and nudity. Even the martyrdom of the early Christian, thrown to the lions, was treated as a public show. This aspect of theatre must form part of our total picture, because so much entertainment has been based on it. At different times, people have watched fighting and killing for sport, indulging in pastimes where animals were, or are still, killed, such as bear-baiting, cock-fighting, bullfighting and fox-hunting, as well as watching humans fight, in tournaments, wrestling, boxing and other martial sports. Even public executions have sometimes been enjoyed as a popular show; during the French Revolution crowds stood by to watch people being guillotined. One way in which violence is made less brutal is in competitive games, such as football, or games of mental conflict, such as chess. Another way is through drama, when actors simply pretend to kill each other.

Plays are often based on conflict, either physical, mental or emotional. Excitement and pleasure are created by the suspense and changing tensions between opposing forces, whether that opposition is between human beings, between human beings and gods, or within human beings themselves. Conflict, crisis and resolution is often the shape that dramatic action takes. The play is not over until that action is complete, whether or not physical violence has been shown.

The question of violence in drama is controversial. Arguments rage about the amount of violence shown on television. Some people believe that drama provides a healthy outlet for aggressive feelings. This viewpoint is old as well as modern. The Greek critic, Aristotle, wrote that drama purged the emotions. But others believe that seeing physical violence encourages people to use it themselves.

The same questions arise over the presentation of sex in the theatre. Whether an audience is moved by a love scene, screaming over a pop idol, or watching pornography, sexual pleasure often forms part of the enjoyment. It is difficult to draw a dividing line between harmless pleasure and titillation or exploitation. For example, some feminists disapprove of beauty contests, while many people cannot understand their condemnation of what seems a harmless event. Thus popular theatre presents certain problems to the authorities in any community. For that reason, censorship of drama has often been practised.

Censorship

Censorship may be imposed in the theatre for several reasons, each of which has been used at various times. The first reason is disapproval of the whole idea of theatre. The Greek philosopher, Plato, would have banned theatre in his ideal republic, because it was basically a pretence, a falsehood. His ideas were not put into practice in his society, but they have had considerable influence in the Western World. In Judaism, the second commandment ('Thou shalt not make false idols') can be understood to forbid, or at least to limit, the art of theatre. The Christian Church banned drama for many years. After the Reformation in the sixteenth century, Puritans reimposed the ban wherever, and whenever, they had sufficient influence. The Moslem religion also disapproved of theatre; its development was therefore slower in the Arab world, where Islamic control of culture was strongest.

A second reason for imposing censorship is when drama threatens the established authority in any community. Popular comedy exaggerates and criticises faults; it often turns the world topsy turvy. For example, in the Roman Catholic Church, a popular feast-day evolved amongst clerics, called the Feast of Fools, in which an ass was led in procession through the church, and the people were pelted with black puddings and sausages instead of incense. This parody of the normal church service might have endangered the authority of the established bishops, but they appeared to have tolerated it. In many societies, these occasional entertainments which 'knock' the official regime are accepted as a kind of end-of-term joke, enjoyed by all as a temporary release from normal rules. But if the authority of the regime is under threat, then such ridicule is not so easily tolerated. Indeed, in an unstable regime, all drama may be censored. You will find that the more totalitarian regimes impose heavy restrictions on drama. For example, in modern Greece, during the Colonels' regime of the 1960s, censorship was strict, and in the Soviet Union, all the arts have usually had to conform to approved form and content.

In Europe, where the politics of each nation have changed several times, the history of censorship provides a scale by which one can measure the strength and confidence of various monarchies and governments. For example, in Shakespeare's time, he and his company were once arrested for performing his play *Richard II*. This was because it depicted a monarch who was usurped, and Queen Elizabeth I at that time feared a rebellion in her own country. It was no use pleading that the play was about a different monarch. 'Know ye not I am Richard II?' she demanded of her advisors. But both before and after this, those who have wished to criticise the ruling authority have often done it through theatre, veiling their attack through the disguise of drama.

Other reasons for censoring drama are to prevent brutality and obscenity. Theatre is open to both these vices, because violence and sex are an integral part of drama, whether they are physically present or not. It is not easy, however, to decide when the bounds of morality and decency have been overstepped, but many governments have taken responsibility for just that kind of decision.

In England, from 1660, when theatre was reintroduced after the Puritan ban, until 1843, only two London theatres were officially allowed to present drama. When this strict law was lifted (and it had been extremely difficult to enforce), every new play had to be submitted to the Lord Chamberlain's office before being publicly performed. This law, which became a tedious bureaucratic chore to regulate, was finally lifted in 1968, liberating drama for the first time in over three hundred years.

Performance and text

This last method of regulating theatre depended on a specialised interpretation of what a play is. It was the text or script which had to be submitted to the Lord Chamberlain, consisting of the words which were to be spoken, together with the stage directions, that is, a written description of the actions. However, theatre events are performances of plays, which are not the same thing as written texts. Plays arose out of story-telling, ritual and mimicry. They were performed through speech, gesture, song and dance, and handed on through oral tradition and imitation. However, as writing came to be important in world culture, history and instructions could be passed on in written form, while stories, plays and poetry became literature as well as performance art. Once the creation of a play became separated out into performance and text, two distinct roles emerged, the actor and the playwright. The text of a play is often the strongest piece of evidence that survives about a performance, and an important tool in recreating a performance. For this reason, the history of theatre has depended heavily on the study of play texts. Many theatre histories have really been histories of dramatic literature. But to study theatre through the history of its drama is to distort one's view, because only a fraction of the dramas that have been performed survive as texts. Hundreds of Greek plays were performed, but less than fifty texts have come down to us, by a circuitous route from Greece to the Arab world and then back to Europe. The plays performed by *commedia* troupes in Italy were not completely written down, because the improvisational nature of the performance was one of its most important characteristics. A written play text is an incomplete version of a play. It is either a way of recording what was performed for posterity, in the same way that a report of a meeting records what happened; or it provides instructions for actors and production team about what is to be created, as an architect creates a blueprint to be followed in constructing a building.

During the twentieth century, people have gradually recognised that we must look at all aspects of theatre to gain a clear impression of what was done. Anthropology and archaeology have helped to widen the scope of theatre history, while transport and communications have allowed more interchange of performance and design. Before the twentieth century, Eastern drama seemed quaint to Europeans, because they did not understand in what context plays had been performed. And until recently, Western historians tended to ignore indigenous African theatre, defining theatre as a written text performed by actors on a stage with scenery.

Much early drama was anonymous, but in each society where plays began to be written down, the names of authors became known as well. In examining play texts, we are usually looking at the work of a single person, who has provided a group of actors with a draft script. As with architectural blueprints, the finished work – the performance – may differ from the original plans. Sometimes these adjustments are noted, and the text is altered. It is therefore interesting to discover, if possible, whether a text you are studying was completed before performance or afterwards. If it was before performance, it is to some extent untested, and must be regarded as a sort of prescription, which could be changed if it did not work. During the rehearsal period of a play, most companies prepare a prompt copy, which is a master copy of the script, containing a record of the spoken text, the stage directions and the technical instructions, such as warnings and cues for lighting, sound, scene changes and performers' entrances. This is valuable, both for repeat performances and for histories.

A play text, then, is not usually complete in itself, as a

poem or a novel is, but is a written prescription for, or description of, a performance. Exceptions to these definitions are plays written to be read, rather than performed. This kind of play is called closet drama. A famous example is John Milton's dramatic poem, *Samson Agonistes* (1671), which was composed like a play text, but which the author envisaged being performed purely mentally, in the imagination of the reader. Such plays do not form a part of the study of theatre, unless, as happened with this example, they are, at some time, performed.

The vast number of playscripts which have survived is but a fraction of the number which have been performed worldwide through the centuries. It forms a treasure-house for us to delve into today, and in that treasure-house are several storeys and many rooms. What follows is a personal anthology of plays from before the seventeenth century, as a possible starting point for a study of dramatic literature. Each one chosen is unique to itself and also an example of a particular kind of drama.

Selection of pre-seventeenth century dramatic literature

Antigone, an example of Greek tragedy
This play was first performed in about 442 BCE in Athens. It was by Sophocles, one of the three great tragedians of ancient Greece (the other two being Aeschylus and Euripides). The Greeks had developed a huge range of myths and legends which formed the basis of their plays. This one was drawn from stories about the city of Thebes. The heroine is Antigone, who wants to bury her brother, but is forbidden to do so by Creon, her uncle, who is King. She insists on disobeying Creon, although her brother had attacked the city. Creon punishes her by shutting her up in a cave, but his own son, who loves Antigone, commits suicide. The story, simple in outline, was set in the context of what had happened to Oedipus, Antigone's father and Creon's brother-in-law. Oedipus had brought a curse on the city by unknowingly killing his father and marrying his own mother. Creon was trying to restore stability to the city after Oedipus's self-exile.

There were many aspects of the story that related to taboos and rites for the dead, practised in different form by all communities. Sophocles put the emphasis on the different stands taken by Antigone and Creon in answering the demands of the dead and of the living. Although the confrontation between protagonist and antagonist seems at first sight to be very simple, the richness of the drama becomes clearer when we start to consider on how many different levels they met: as members of the same family, mourning another member, as woman and man, as subject and ruler, as young and old.

The play has been translated and adapted many times. One adaptation was by a modern French playwright, Jean Anouilh, who emphasised Antigone's role as someone who simply has to say 'no', without having a rational explanation for her refusal to obey. His version was first performed in 1943 when France was occupied by the Nazis. There was an underlying parallel between Antigone and the Resistance movement.

The Menaechmi, an example of Roman comedy

This play was written by Plautus and produced in Rome after 184 BCE. It tells the story of identical twin boys who were separated in childhood but land up in the same city, where much confusion occurs before their real identities are revealed. This slender story gave the opportunity for many ridiculous situations and misunderstandings to be explored, and was therefore an excellent vehicle for comic acting, such as mime artists and *commedia* troupes excelled in. Shakespeare used the play as the basis for his *Comedy of Errors*, in which he compounded the confusion by making the twins' servants another pair of identical twins. He used twins in *Twelfth Night* too. Many other writers have exploited the comic possibilities, including Jean Anouilh, mentioned above, in *L'Invitation au Chateau* (*Ring Round the Moon*), where the same actor played both twins. Another adaptation was an American musical comedy, *The Boys from Syracuse*. The idea of twins, and of mistaken identity, fascinates us because it makes us examine the whole question of individuality, and what makes each person different.

Sakoontala, an example of early Indian drama
This play was written in Sanskrit, the literary language of
India, by Kalidasa (?375–?415), the author of at least two
other plays. The hero is a king who meets Sakoontala, the
beautiful daughter of a hermit and a nymph. They fall in
love and marry secretly, but a curse is laid upon them,
making the king forget her and the marriage. Sakoontala
loses the ring by which the king is destined to recognise her,
but eventually the ring is found, and they are reunited, with
the son she has borne him, who is destined to become one of
the greatest kings.

This romantic story is one of the best known Sanskrit
dramas in the rest of the world. It was performed during the
golden age of Hindu theatre (between about 120 and 500 CE).
Like the Greeks, the Indians developed a whole collection of
myths and legends from which this story was drawn. It had
many of the elements of traditional fairy tales. We can trace
similarities to stories all over the world, including *The Arabian
Nights*. In romance of this kind, the emphasis was on the
forces of good, represented here by the god Indra and his
assistants, who helped bring the virtuous characters through
hardship to eventual happiness, just as the fairy godmother
did in *Cinderella*. The idea of kingship also featured, for King
Dunyasha had responsibilities to the community and to the
heavenly powers, as well as to Sakoontala.

The Chalk Circle, an example of Chinese drama
This play was written and produced in North China,
probably during the Yuan period, between 1279 and 1368.
The heroine is a young woman called Hai-T'ang, who
becomes the second wife of a rich lord, Ma Chun-sking, and
bears him a son. The first wife poisons Lord Ma in order to
marry her lover, and puts the blame on Hai-T'ang. She also
appropriates Hai-T'ang's son, because he is Lord Ma's heir.
The case against Hai-T'ang is eventually tried by a high
judge, who gives the two mothers the 'chalk circle' test,
putting the child in the middle and saying that the true
mother will draw him out. When Hai-T'ang refuses to hurt
the child, the judge recognises her as the true mother.

In China, the chief cultural influences were Confucianism
and Taoism. Confucianism emphasised the importance of

morality and of a defined social order; Taoism emphasised the paradoxical nature of life. (If one intends to achieve something, he starts with its opposite, and if he wants to retain anything, he admits into it something of its opposite.) Much of Chinese drama revolved round ethics and social conduct, especially the hierarchy of family life, which was the pivot of Chinese society.

The Chalk Circle shows a complex society where almost all the power resides in money and reputation. Yet in that play, virtue and justice triumph. Why? Was it because that was true to life? Or was it because showing that in a play would encourage the practice of virtue and courage? Was the play meant to console the audience through a happy pretence? Or was it by then a convention that plays should end happily? These questions about happy and sad endings still arise, and audiences have to judge for themselves the truth and validity of any play's conclusion.

This story of the wise judge is very like the judgement of Solomon in the Old Testament, where the test of the true mother was the threat to cut the child in two. Such stories may have been widespread. Here the emphasis was on the great suffering the heroine had to endure at the hands of a corrupt woman. The story was used again in *The Caucasian Chalk Circle* by the German playwright Bertolt Brecht, in 1945. Brecht gave the story an extra twist by having a corrupt but likeable judge give the child, not to the natural mother, but to the maid who had nursed it and cared for it.

Nakamitsu, an example of Japanese *Noh*

This play was probably written and produced in the early fifteenth century. It was by Zeami, the greatest of the *Noh* playwrights. The hero, Nakamitsu, is servant to a lord, and each has a son. The lord, in a fit of anger against his son, tells Nakamitsu to kill him. Instead, Nakamitsu sacrifices his own son. Eventually, the truth is revealed and the lord receives back his son.

While the characters were specifically Japanese, belonging to the strict feudal and military regime of the Shogunate, this compact story opened up themes of divided loyalty, sacrifice and forgiveness which many other cultures had dealt with.

In the Judaic-Christian tradition, Abraham was ready to sacrifice his son Isaac for God, but was saved at the last moment. One of Christ's parables dealt with the father who forgave the prodigal son. Shakespeare put into one of his history plays the double situation of a father killing his son, and a son killing his father, in civil war. Any culture which taught the double duty of loyalty to family and to a higher lord or law, threw up stories of this kind.

Everyman, an example of medieval Christian drama
The English version of this play corresponded to a Flemish play, printed in 1495. Both were anonymous products of pre-Reformation Catholic Europe. God sends Death to summon Everyman to a reckoning. Everyman tries to persuade various characters of earthly life to accompany him on his journey, including Fellowship and Worldly Goods. Only Good Deeds, who is very weak, agrees to go with him, and Knowledge, who takes him to Confession where he receives absolution for his sins. He is then ready to meet Death, but has to take leave of various characters of earthly qualities, including Beauty and Strength. Finally, he goes to his grave and an angel leads him up towards Heaven.

This story was an allegory of Christian repentance and salvation. Although it taught a specifically Catholic lesson, it had dramatic elements which went far beyond those limits. One element was the typically medieval image of life as a journey, an image which influenced much literature, including John Bunyan's *Pilgrim's Progress* (printed in 1678), Henrik Ibsen's *Peer Gynt* (1867), and August Strindberg's *Road to Damascus* (1898). Another element was the inevitable confrontation with Death, which was dramatised in many stories and dramas.

Dr Faustus, an example of Renaissance drama
This play was written by Christopher Marlowe and performed in London in the 1590s. The hero, Dr Faustus, sells his soul to the devil, Mephistopheles, in return for twenty-four years of magical power, at the end of which he goes to hell.

The story came from a German tale. Its chief interest lay in its exploration of the limits of human power, and the temptation to increase that power by evil means. The most famous adaptation was by the German playwright, Goethe, who wrote two long versions (*Faust I* and *II*, published in 1808 and 1832) which explored the philosophical implications of the story. Lighthearted versions of the story dealt with the choices people made when they could have anything they wished. For example, in a film version, *Bedazzled*, the hero tried to wish for happiness with the woman he loved, but kept getting the wish wrong. The serious aspects of the theme were dealt with in stories showing what limitless power was like when handled immorally or destructively. For example, in *Frankenstein* and other science fiction.

The period when Marlowe's *Dr Faustus* was written and performed was when European culture began to move forward towards a position of power and influence over other cultures. It was a period of expansion, both physical and intellectual, bringing about changes in drama as well as in other arts. Marlowe captured some of the aspirations of Renaissance men as they became aware of their own potential. How much of knowledge, wisdom and desire was obtainable? That was the question Faustus asked. Although he was taught a terrible lesson through aspiring too high, others in the same era were questioning what had seemed the most basic truths of humanity. It was the age of Copernicus, Galileo and Kepler, who changed the whole concept of the universe and its laws, as understood by men and women of the time.

The expanding world of drama

This was the age when the world which had centred on Rome began to break up, expanding in different forms, just as the continents themselves had done when the lands were being formed. There was the exploration and settlement of the New World; there was the fragmentation of Catholic Christianity, which split into various forms of Protestantism and the Roman Catholic Church; there was the invention and development of the printing press; there was the discovery that the earth moved round the sun; there was the revival of classical arts and learning, called the Renaissance, or rebirth. As the medieval period ended, the civilisation of Western Europe did not decline or become static as many other civilisations had done, but reformed, as its Church did, expanded and gradually achieved dominance. The explosion and expansion of ideas was reflected in all the European arts, and was manifested in the extraordinary flowering of theatre in England during Marlowe's and Shakespeare's time, as well as in Italy, Spain, Portugal and France during those crucial hundred years or so. An important change, as far as dramatic literature was concerned, was the spread of texts and commentaries through the printed word.

Until the development of the printing press, the written word was exclusive to a few people. Repetition of words was predominantly oral. Monks laboured long, copying out precious manuscripts, but the spreading and popularising of words was done through performance and repetition, the essence of theatre. When books became cheaper and easier to come by, what must the effect have been on the drama? Must not some people have worried that the printed word would rival the spoken word and wipe out theatre, just as, in a later age, it was feared that cinema, radio and television might? It did not, any more than those modern media did, but it altered the place of drama in the culture, raising the dramatic text to a special place of honour, and allowing the development of new functions, those of the dramatic critic and the historian of drama.

Dramatic criticism in Europe

Greek drama was known in Rome, and the Renaissance spread classical learning throughout Europe, supplemented by new texts which came to Europe via the Arab world. These texts included the earliest surviving work of dramatic theory, Aristotle's *Poetics*, which described and analysed many of the chief characteristics of Greek tragedy. What he wrote on comedy was lost, but the *Poetics* came to be used as a prescription for neo-classical tragedy, and remains a perceptive study of dramatic form.

Roman criticism was partly derived from Aristotle, and in typically Roman style, it tidied up some of the loose ends. Neo-classical critics then prescribed three *unities* for drama and developed a list of categories, which Shakespeare ridiculed in *Hamlet*, when he had the pompous character

Polonius defining: 'tragedy, comedy, history, pastoral, pastoral-comical, historical-pastoral, tragical-historical, tragical-comical-historical-pastoral, scene individable or poem unlimited' (Act II, Scene ii, l. 396).

Another work on theatre existed, the *Natya Sustra, Doctrine of Dramatic Art*, written in India several hundred years before the Renaissance. If it had been known in Europe, the gulf between Eastern and Western theatre might not have been so great in the next few hundred years.

The great medieval dramas were the other models for Shakespeare and his contemporaries. The playwrights of the Corpus Christi plays did not distinguish different kinds of drama, but got their effects through mingling the serious and the comic, the sacred and the secular. Shakespeare followed this recipe, but shaped his plays into the neo-classical approved five acts. Seventeenth-century critics of Shakespeare found themselves forced to disapprove of him. For instance, John Dryden pointed out that he did not stick to the prescribed rules of drama, but still he could not help praising Shakespeare's 'native woodnotes wild'.

French seventeenth-century dramatists followed most closely the 'rules' of neo-classical drama. Their plays kept to the three unities of time, place and action: the length of time covered by the story to be about twenty-four hours; the action to take place in the same location; the action to be a single story without subplots. Two tragic writers, Corneille and Racine, and one comic, Molière, used this form to great effect, and many other writers disciplined their work into this strict form. Critics in England still had to contend with the fact that Shakespeare's plays were popular but his scenes shifted vast distances – between Egypt and Rome, for example, in *Antony and Cleopatra*; that he sometimes covered a huge span of time – jumping sixteen years, for example, in *The Winter's Tale*; and that he introduced plots to complement the main action, in *King Lear*, for example, where the story of a king and his three daughters was intercut with the story of the Duke of Gloucester and his two sons. Also, Shakespeare did not seem to be able to make up his mind if he was writing tragedy or comedy, putting comic characters into even the starkest tragedies, such as the Porter in *Macbeth*.

Tragedy and comedy

The distinction between tragedy and comedy remained important in defining European drama, and was, as it happened, paralleled by the *Noh* and *Kyogen* forms in Japan. Tragic characters were dignified, high-ranking and influential, with no reference made to their baser needs, while comic characters were middle or lower class, powerful only in their households, and showing all the incongruities and idiosyncrasies of mankind, placed on the scale of creation between gross animals and noble images of the gods.

The distinction between tragedy and comedy arose from the way a story was treated rather than from the subject matter, even though some situations might seem to lean entirely towards one or the other. For example, the subject of adultery has been turned into both tragedy and comedy. To illustrate this point two French plays of the seventeenth century have been selected, both written when dramatic critics held considerable power over the theatre.

Tartuffe, an example of French comedy
This play by Molière (1664) is a comedy in which the main character, who wants to be thought virtuous and holy, is unmasked as a hypocrite because of his ungovernable lust towards the wife of the man he has been duping. The scenes where he approaches the wife are highly comical and physical.

Phèdre, an example of neo-classical French tragedy
This play by Jean Racine, written in 1677, is a tragedy in which the main character has an ungovernable passion for her stepson, Hippolyte. Her suffering provides the basis of the tragedy, which ends in her death and Hippolyte's. The drama is conducted in formal, poetic language, often reaching levels of great intensity.

During the eighteenth century, plays began to develop that were neither pure tragedy nor comedy, stretching the powers of critics, who then defined the sentimental comedy and the pathetic tragedy, forcing one playwright to describe his comedy as a laughing comedy to avoid misunderstanding. These new distinctions were created, not because writers were mixing tragedy and comedy as Shakespeare had done, but because they were exploring the middle ground between the two, especially the interaction between different classes in society. Here are two examples:

She Stoops To Conquer, an example of eighteenth-century comedy
This play, written by Oliver Goldsmith in 1773 is the laughing comedy just referred to. In it, the heroine pretends to be a maid, in order to encourage her suitor who is too shy to court a lady.

The Marriage of Figaro, an example of social comedy
This play was written in 1784 by Pierre Augustin Caron de Beaumarchais. It is a comedy of masters and servants, a traditional form since Roman times. The *commedia* troupes had used the form and Molière had perfected it, showing situations where servants mocked their masters. Here it was turned into a criticism of high society, and for that reason it was censored, written as it was only five years before the French Revolution. In 1786 it passed the censor and gained immense popularity when turned into an opera by Mozart.

Some writers in Europe, and in the American colonies as well, were beginning to look at society from a different point of view, seeing more tragic struggles going on at the lower levels than at the upper. The drama of revolution was beginning, which aimed to change the way society looked at itself. The static forms of tragedy and comedy might have to go. The volatile form of opera assumed importance (see Chapter 8). Here are two examples of revolutionary drama.

A Doll's House
This play, by the Norwegian playwright Henrik Ibsen, was first performed in Copenhagen in 1879, after being written in Italy. The heroine is Nora, who has borrowed money without telling her husband, because he needs expensive medical treatment. Despite all her secret efforts, she is unable to repay it. Her husband discovers the 'crime' and rejects her. When the creditor decides to forgive the debt, the husband

forgives Nora, but she is no longer willing to live as his wife, and leaves their home and children.

The story is told in such a way that deeper layers of truth about the past and present are gradually revealed. What had seemed a happy marriage, with a strong husband supporting a pretty, carefree little wife, is eventually shown to be a sham, no more real than life in a doll's house. Although Nora is a wife and mother, she has not been trained to become a mature adult. She has to leave her husband and children in order to have the chance to become one.

In the hundred years of its life, *A Doll's House* has become an important play, performed throughout the world, especially in Europe and America, but also in Japan and other parts of Asia. It can arouse strong emotions and fierce controversy in any community unsure about the stability of marriage as a social institution.

The Cherry Orchard

This play by Anton Chekhov was first performed in Moscow in 1904, directed by Konstantin Stanislavsky. It is about an impoverished aristocratic family who reluctantly sell their cherry orchard to a landowner to build a housing estate. A number of smaller incidents are built around this central one, all contributing to an underlying story of change in Russian society as the power moves away from the few at the top.

There is no single hero, heroine or villain in the play. Chekhov focused on a whole group of different characters, dramatising the relationships in the household with a mixture of poignancy and comedy, so that he showed the complicated pattern and ambiguous situation of the community. Chekhov intended his plays to be comedies, but Stanislavsky preferred to treat them as tragedy. At the time, the play was a prediction of the Russian revolution, which was imminent. It has continued to be a powerful evocation of society in a state of flux, with sympathy balanced between the old civilisation that was dying, and the new that was being born. Thus, although the story was not based on any myth, it followed the mythical pattern of death and rebirth which has been so important in the rhythm of drama.

European forms of drama were fluid. Not for long did the playwrights allow their work to be prescribed within set limits. The developing traditions were unbroken from medieval times onwards, but combined, at the time of the Renaissance, with earlier classical forms. Something was pushing the drama forward. Sometimes one aspect of theatre was predominant, sometimes another. Ibsen's work was written away from the country he wrote about, and produced elsewhere; Chekhov's plays failed until Stanislavsky found a way to present them – or thought he did. Perhaps that something was the sense of drama in European life itself. Nations and societies were being created, on show for others to see. An important motif that appeared and reappeared in European drama, was the theatre's sense of itself.

The idea of theatre in plays

In many of Shakespeare's plays, the characters themselves perform a play. In *Hamlet*, for instance, a play is performed which is an imitation of what had recently happened at the Danish court. Hamlet has discovered that his father the king was murdered by his uncle, who then married his mother, the queen. He organises the presentation at court of a play in which these incidents are acted. This creates a complicated series of mirror images of actors and spectators.

The scene is Act III Scene ii of *Hamlet*. In the real theatre, the spectators are watching actors performing *Hamlet*. On the stage the characters consist of courtiers and players. There is a King and a Player King. There is a Queen and a Player Queen. Hamlet is watching the king. Some of the courtiers are watching Hamlet instead of the play. The crux of the scene rests on what the king and queen are watching. The actors themselves may be watching the spectators as well as each other. For all we know the spectators are watching each other as well.

Shakespeare was not alone in finding that the image of the theatre stimulated exciting thoughts about the human condition. The motto of the Globe Playhouse was 'Totus mundus agit histrionem', which loosely translated into Shakespeare's own line: 'All the world's a stage'. In *Hamlet* he wrote that the purpose of playing was 'to hold, as 'twere the mirror up to nature'. The theatre, as Shakespeare and his contemporaries saw it, was a drama within a drama, a small world within a larger world. This idea fitted into their whole view of man, the world and the universe. For they pictured the whole of life in terms of worlds within worlds, which influenced each other. Man was a microcosm or little world, containing within himself all the elements of the real world, be it the natural world, or society as a whole. The universe was a macrocosm or large world, containing the same elements enlarged.

Gradually, the idea of how man saw him/herself changed, especially as scientific knowledge increased. From the time of Galileo to Einstein, progress and change in Europe was characterised not only by social movements already described, but by the growth of knowledge gained empirically, that is by observation, through the invention of instruments like the telescope and microscope, and through the systematic, objective analysis of the information obtained. In this way, a picture of the universe was created which was orderly and mechanical, and obeyed the laws of nature. It depended on the scientist developing his/her objectivity so that he/she did not distort scientific facts. A scientific method was developed in which an experiment could be set up in known, repeatable conditions. The results of that experiment were considered as proof for or against the theory being tested.

This experimental method was paralleled in the arts by the development of naturalism in the nineteenth century. Some painters, for example, instead of depicting mythical characters and scenes of beauty, began to turn to the world they observed around them, recording it as they saw it, often revealing pain, poverty and squalor more vividly than had been customary. Some novelists, too, such as Emile Zola in France, described the observable quality of life, documenting it for their contemporaries and for posterity. The invention of the camera was particularly important to the scientific method, allowing visual observation and recording to become mechanical. This naturalistic movement extended into the theatre, turning the whole audience into a group of observers. The plays of Ibsen and Chekhov, for example had naturalistic features, presenting stories taken from observable contemporary society, not legend, and characters who behaved to a great extent as people did in ordinary life, not as heroes, heroines, villains or gods.

It was never possible, of course, for theatrical observation to become mechanical, though the camera was quickly developed to record movement as well as static views, leading to the development of the cinema. Theatre was too emotional and volatile. It was a better vehicle for change and revolution than for cool observation. Naturalistic art was closely linked with the need for social reform. Naturalistic theatre provided a platform for reformers, such as the Irish playwright Bernard Shaw, who was a Socialist.

No sooner had innovative European playwrights discovered naturalism, than they felt the need to break away from it. One of the ways to do so was to remind themselves and the audience of what had begun to be forgotten: that in the live theatre, there is no clearcut distinction between the actors and the audience; that observation and participation are not as different as scientists were leading people to believe. At the same time, physicists such as Albert Einstein were discovering for themselves that the scientist could not leave him/herself out of an experiment when seeking to discover the truth. The observer affected the experiment, just as the audience affected the drama in a theatre. There follows an example of a play where theatre and life were seen to overlap.

Six Characters In Search Of An Author
This Italian play, written in 1921 by Luigi Pirandello, begins with a company of actors rehearsing a play. They are interrupted by the arrival of six people who claim to be 'characters' and wish to have their drama played out. They represent a family which has painfully split and been reunited. Because of the separation, the father does not recognise his own stepdaughter when he meets her again, and only just avoids using her as a prostitute. At the end, the youngest child drowns, guilt for her death being apportioned through the family. We see in this story some of the same basic dramatic patterns of guilt, remorse and family relationships, but set in a context which makes the theatre itself the subject of the play.

The beginning of the play is a joke against naturalistic theatre, showing that you could not put the reality of this family drama on the stage. For example, the Producer tries to make the Stepdaughter speak louder, so that she can be heard, but she protests 'Louder? Louder? What are you talking about? These aren't matters which can be shouted at the top of one's voice.' The play develops like a philosophical debate: which are the *real* people in the play? Those who claim to be real but who seem fragmentary and superficial? Or the 'characters' whose psychological truth is deeper, and who are fixed for all time in their own drama?

This play helped to give back to the theatre that powerful double metaphor it had had in Shakespeare's time. Not only did a play reflect the world, but the world itself was a kind of theatre, and what happened in it was like a play. In the modern world, the television screen shows us events of world drama in news programmes and documentaries, as well as through scripted plays. But live theatre, too, continues to play its part in modern culture.

Plays in the modern world

The spread of the printed word has meant that there now exists a huge repertoire of world drama, easily available to any theatre group. Foreign and historical plays can be put on, either in the style in which they were originally performed, or else adapted to the needs of a different time or place. More importantly, for the creation of new plays, rich and varied sources of drama can be studied and experienced. A Greek tragedy might inspire a play of social protest in South America or an African ritual drama; while in Central America, a theatre group might turn to Mayan and Aztec traditions to create its identity anew. The German playwright Bertolt Brecht used Chinese drama as a basis for his *Good Person of Szechwan*, while W. B. Yeats was influenced by Japanese *Noh* plays. In India, at the same time, the philosopher, writer and teacher Rabindranath Tagore set out to unify Indian and European traditions, creating plays which have been described as a mixture of Bengali folk drama and western medieval mystery plays. In Europe, as world domination has begun to crumble, the drama has sometimes reflected feelings of disillusionment, in response to the loss of confidence in the old political and religious values.

Yet this disillusionment has sometimes been expressed in inspiring drama, leading one critic to coin the term 'theatre of the absurd'. There follows an example of this kind of post-war European drama.

Endgame
This play was written in French in 1957 by the Irish playwright Samuel Beckett, and first performed in London. The main characters are Hamm, who is blind and sits in a chair in the centre of the stage, and Clov, who waits on him, and tells him of the bleak world outside the room they are in. Two other characters, Nagg and Nell, are an old couple living in two dustbins in the room. The characters are playing out their last moves in the game of living; outside, the world seems to be coming to an end too.

There is no real story to the play. The title reveals that it is about the end of something. It could be the end of the world, or the end of civilisation, or the end of the play that Hamm and Clov have been acting out. The play captures a sense of futility and despair which characterised a part of the spirit of Western civilisation after the Second World War, with its holocaust and its atom bombs. The characters seem to be fools or madmen, yet their behaviour seems the wisest response to the meaningless world in which they find themselves. The play is not tragic, but the blackest of comedies, with laughter and despair going hand in hand.

In many non-European countries, the search for a new drama has reflected the search for a new post-colonial identity. First, European plays and styles were imported. Then, in many countries, a reaction against colonialism led to the encouragement of indigenous forms of drama. New drama sometimes combined indigenous and European techniques to address the problems and questions raised by today's interbred culture. Here is one example of a modern African play.

Death and the King's Horseman
This play was written in England in 1974, by the Nigerian playwright Wole Soyinka. Set in an ancient Yoruba city, in the last years of British colonial rule, it tells the story of

Elesin Oba and his eldest son, Olunde. Elesin is to die by
Yoruba custom, because the king has died and he is his
horseman. On the eve of his death he chooses to take another
man's bride as his wife and pours his seed into her body.
Because she saps his strength, and/or because the District
Officer imprisons him and prevents his suicide, to his shame,
he survives his destined moment. His son Olunde, sent to
medical school in England by the District Officer, returns to
witness his father's disgrace. He kills himself, fulfilling the
rite his father has failed to perform.

On one level, the play is a comparison of British and
Yoruba values. But it is more importantly about transition –
from one culture to another, from life to death, and from
death to life. The British way of life is shown to be as
decadent and retrogressive as the Yoruba way, despite that
preoccupation with ritual death. But Olunde's self-sacrifice is
born out of what he has learnt to admire in British courage
and ethics, as well as out of his sense of duty to his father's
values.

Drawing on the double tradition of Western and African
rites and theatrical language, Soyinka blended them into a
play in which, as in Greek and Shakespearean tragedy, the
welfare of a community was damaged, life and death were
wasted, but at the end there was hope of renewal, and
reconciliation in the next generation.

Thus drama continues to reflect the micro/macrocosm as
it did in Shakespeare's time. Where drama once reflected the
beliefs of a local community, now it may set those beliefs in
the context of a world community, helping each individual
member of the audience find his/her place in it. Amongst
others, the playwright, too, has to discover his/her appropriate
role.

The playwright's role

For the student of theatre, the printed play is often the most
important artefact. But it is actually a by-product of theatre.
Shakespeare's contemporary, Ben Jonson, took pride in the
works he had created and had them published. Ever since
then, the dramatic poet has been able to see his/her works in
print, and be known by many who have never stepped inside

a theatre. The printed play, with its author's name beneath the title, may make us forget that a play is a collaborative effort. In the business of making a piece of theatre, the writer's role does not always take priority. The script is sometimes radically transformed in rehearsal, performance and revival. Many playwrights have been employed as literary hacks, required to turn out whatever material suits the needs of an acting company. Scriptwriters in films and television often find themselves in the same position today, required to produce a screenplay on demand. Even well-known writers have found their status and influence low in the film studio. If their work does not suit the producers, the director or the stars, they may be fired, and someone else brought in to cobble the script together.

Such treatment of writers seems philistine and destructive to those who appreciate the skill required to write a play. But if the playwright's prestige is too much greater than other theatre artists', theatre comes to be regarded as a purely literary and intellectual pursuit. During the centuries in Europe when dramatic criticism developed, popular theatre was largely ignored by historians and critics. The knockabout, mainly unscripted, styles of theatre probably continued in an unbroken tradition from Roman times and perhaps earlier, a poor relation to the legitimate theatre. One branch developed to become circus; another became vaudeville, music-hall and variety; another, street entertainment, called *guignol* in France, and typified in Punch and Judy shows in Britain; another branch became the traditional British Christmas pantomime. When Europeans first came to appreciate black African theatre in the twentieth century, they were encountering a tradition in which no distinction existed between popular and elitist theatre. In Asian theatre they saw traditions in which gesture, movement and colour were regarded as being at least as profound as the spoken word. In the Peking Opera of China, for example, the performances dominate the theatre so much that the names of dramatists are not even listed in the programmes. In the twentieth century, some have sought for what they call total or synthetic theatre, where sound and vision are bound together in a seamless whole. The playwright's role is an ever changing one, as scripted words gain or lose predominance in the art of theatre.

7

The scenic effect

WE now come to an aspect of theatre that could be largely
dispensed with, and yet is at the same time so intriguing that
it is virtually an art in itself – the creation of the scenic effect.
As we have seen, the essential needs are time, space, actor
and audience for the creation of a play. The actor uses
his/her powers to awaken the audience's imagination. The
more the actors take on the role of story-tellers, the more
vividly they can conjure up in the mind's eye, either through
their words or their actions, the environment in which the
story takes place. This art can be exerted immediately, at
any time and in any space. The first few lines of *Romeo and
Juliet*, for instance, set the scene and the situation very
swiftly:

> Two households, both alike in dignity
> In fair Verona, where we lay our scene,
> From ancient grudge break to new mutiny.
>
> (Act I, Scene i, l. 1)

But there is also the prepared art of creating the environment
physically and setting it in place as a replica of the real
world. Both these arts belong to theatre, sometimes working
together to create a lifelike illusion for the audience/spectators,
sometimes rivalling each other in impressiveness, sometimes
deliberately made to contrast with each other.

Scenery, props and lighting

There are three elements used in creating the visual effect
required in the theatre. One is the scenery which has been
set up on the stage to create the appropriate surroundings.
Another word used for it is the set. We also talk about the

setting for a story, meaning the time and place in which it occurs. (For example 'The scene is laid in Cornwall . . .' or 'Our story is set amidst the rugged scenery of . . . etc.') In the theatre, the set is the scenic background and surroundings for the play.

The stage background and surroundings may be an accurate replica of the place where the play is supposed to occur. However, as with costume, a festive element is also important. The stage is often dressed up decoratively, and so another word that is used is stage décor, putting the emphasis on the adornment of the stage area.

Closely related to scenery are properties. This word, usually shortened to props, is the theatrical term for the countless objects that need to be brought on to the stage and used during the course of the play, ranging from a cigarette lighter in a modern play, to a weapon such as sword, dagger or gun, or an important object like the olive branch in the story of Noah. In writing or talking about theatre, it is not always necessary to distinguish between a prop which is a costume accessory, such as a fan, and a prop which is part of the scenery, such as a cushion or stool. But when it comes to putting on a production, it is very important to know who is responsible for acquiring and placing the prop.

The third element is lighting. Except for performances using only natural daylight, the provision of lighting is always a consideration, ensuring that the audience can see the stage action. Even for daylight performances, lighting must still be taken into account. The play must be timed to fit into daylight hours. The York mystery plays, for example, had to be performed between dawn and dusk. For daylight conditions, the stage must be placed so as to get maximum benefit from the sun. Artificial lighting serves the same basic function, to illuminate the action of the play. Because of technological development, lighting is one of the elements of theatre which has changed most over the centuries. It began its history with candles and oil-lamps, and now uses the resources of sophisticated electrical equipment, which directs and controls the light in a million different ways. In addition to its basic function, lighting can also be used to create or enhance the scenic effect. Even here, natural light can make a contribution. With a little foresight, a performance could be timed to coincide effectively with the setting of the sun. In Chekhov's *The Seagull*, Konstantin tried to time his play to coincide with the rising of the moon. However, moonlight is not very effective for stage lighting. Chekhov was making fun of a naïve attempt to make nature serve the art of theatre.

Although it has been said that the scenic aspect of theatre was largely dispensable, it is important to bear in mind that there is always a stage set and lighting of some form or another, just as there is always costume. The setting may be earth, trees and sky, lit by the sun, yet these natural elements constitute the scenery and lighting for the performance. There are basically three ways of creating the setting and locations required by the story:

to use the real thing;
to construct a scenic illusion of the real thing;
to use signs and symbols of the real thing.

Most theatrical styles call on all these methods, but not mixed equally.

The real thing

Permanent stages sometimes offer the real thing in terms of doors, balconies, stairways and so on. In the Greek theatre, plays were often set outside the palace door, and there was a real stone doorway on the stage. However, everyone knew that it led to backstage, not, for example, to Agamemnon's palace. Although the doorway was real, it was not *the* real doorway. The next day it would become the doorway to some other palace. Thus convention and imagination both contributed to the audience's acceptance of this representation.

One of the most obvious divisions in real space and place is indoor and outdoor. While the Greeks and Romans performed outdoors and set many of their plays outdoors, the Renaissance theatres of Europe varied and so did their scenes. Sometimes an outside scene was played inside, in a hall or indoor theatre; sometimes the open public stage had to represent an interior. The doorways were still real, but the actors' words had to indicate whether the door was supposed to lead from outside to inside or vice versa.

Early Chinese theatres, like Shakespearean public playhouses, were partially roofed, and scenes were set both indoors and outdoors. In Shakespeare's theatre a useful convention was established which allowed the stage to be equally appropriately treated as outside or inside. The stage was roofed, but beneath its canopy were painted the heavens. In *Hamlet*, Shakespeare devised an in-joke with the audience. The hero lamented over his unhappiness, saying that he found no comfort from earth or sky, but the language he used made reference to the *theatrical* representations of earth and sky, that is, the stage and the painted ceiling:

> this goodly *frame*, the earth, seems to me a sterile promontory, this most excellent *canopy* the air, look you, this brave o'erhanging firmament, this majestical *roof fretted* with golden fire, why it appeareth nothing to me but a foul and pestilent congregation of vapours.
>
> (Act II, Scene ii, l. 300)

The italics indicate the significantly theatrical words, referring to the wooden frame of the theatre, the canopy and the carved roof; the last phrase could even be taken as a comic reference to the bad air in the theatre.

It might seem that the best kind of props are real ones, but it is surprising how often the real thing is unsuitable for a theatrical performance. Weapons, whether swords or guns, can be real but must not be harmful. Real food is often surprisingly inappropriate on stage, taking too long to eat, or getting caught in the throat; so substitutes have to be found. A real mirror is often a distraction and has to be dulled with soap. A common question you might hear a stage-manager ask about a piece of scenery or a prop, is 'Is it practical?' which means 'Does it have to *do* what the real thing does?' If not, it may be easier to use something else. An oil-lamp can be real if it does not have to be lit. If it does, it is easier and safer, in the modern theatre, to wire it up to the electric system, and have the actor mime the action of lighting it. Even with electric light on stage, it is rarely the actor's action that turns it on or off. You may be able to think of other examples where the real thing would be inconvenient on stage. Often it takes some ingenuity to make the real thing work on stage. When it does, part of the pleasure is the consciousness of the ingenuity. For example, a famous French production at the end of the nineteenth century put a real butcher's shop upon the stage. The audience found the novelty enjoyable.

The scenic illusion

Into this second category fall some of the most exciting aspects of theatre history. In the Western world, scenic illusion has dominated our whole understanding of what theatre is. From the Renaissance to the beginning of the twentieth century, scenic artists in Europe sought out different ways of creating an illusion of visual reality on the stage. The scenic illusion became an important part of the audience's enjoyment of theatre. In doing this, European theatre followed a path quite different from most Asian theatre, which exploited instead the actors' facility to create images in the minds of the audience.

During the Renaissance, the chief search was for means to create the illusion of perspective on the stage. In painting, the discovery had been made that geometry and trigonometry showed a way of giving the visual illusion of three dimensions by two-dimensional means. It was a considerable feat to adapt this art of seeing into the distance to the stage, which was already three-dimensional. Sometimes it was done through creating the effect of a vista, or view, seen through real arches reminiscent of the classical theatre. Then the art was developed, mainly through an Italian called Sebastiano Serlio (1475–1554), so that the effect of distance was created by a series of screens. Serlio developed three settings which could be adapted for a vast number of scenes in plays. Seeing things in perspective involves seeing things from a particular viewpoint. Scenery had to be placed very precisely for the audience to see only what they were supposed to see. Hence the increasing separation between stage and auditorium during these centuries.

The closer an object is to the horizon, or vanishing point, the smaller it looks. Perspective scenery was set up *behind* the performers. Whenever an actor approached the background, he/she looked like a giant, or a human being in toyland, and the audience had to suspend their disbelief. The art of scene-painting was developed to a high point. The most effective

Serlio's settings for tragic and pastoral scenes

scenery during the eighteenth century was for exterior settings, where the distant landscape was painted on a backcloth, while the middle and foreground were shown on wing drops and borders that framed the action and concealed the offstage areas at the same time. Some scene painters were so skilful they could create the illusion of an interior similarly, using the backcloth to paint one wall, with all its furniture and decorations, while the wing drops and borders were carefully placed and painted, to give the illusion of receding walls.

In the nineteenth century, many plays required an interior. They also required that the actor be able move as if in a real room. The box set was devised, with flats, which were screens supported by iron braces and weights, set around the stage to represent three sides of the room, while the fourth wall was imagined to be within the proscenium arch. In this method, the set was not a real room but looked exactly like one, framed by the proscenium arch. The convention was like that of a still life painting, which looked like the real thing but had a frame which the viewers accepted as a way of separating art from reality. They could admire the ingenuity with which the replica had been made.

Even such realistic innovations were not enough for everyone. In 1888 the Swedish playwright, August Strindberg, complained about scenery where objects are painted on the backcloth: 'Even if the walls have to be of canvas, it is surely

The box set

time to stop painting them with shelves and kitchen utensils'
(From The preface to *Miss Julie*). It was this kind of demand
that led to such productions as the one already mentioned, in
which a butcher's shop was constructed on the stage.

However, Strindberg and André Antoine, who was
responsible for that production, were in danger of forgetting
that the effect of theatre depended on a delicate balance
between reality and illusion. The quest for perfect realism on
the stage will never be fulfilled. But fashions change about
what is acceptable as realism. And just as out-of-date clothes
look crude and comical, so conventions of realism also go out
of style. Nevertheless, the quest for visual realism continued
throughout the nineteenth century, partly because playwrights
and actors wanted to show characters in relation to their
environment, partly because it was fun. A 1904 production of
A Midsummer Night's Dream had real rabbits on the stage.

Although the discovery of perspective had accelerated the
quest for realism, it also created problems. Perspective
scenery had to be designed from a fixed viewpoint. This
meant that not everyone in the theatre had a good view.
Depending on where you were sitting, the sightlines might

spoil the scenic illusion with a view offstage to the side, where scenes and actors were being prepared, or you might see only the tops of the actors' heads. With cinema and television, the camera controls the view, giving every spectator virtually the same sightlines. Such equal rights have made the flaws in scenic realism more apparent. Now the theatre often explores alternatives to realism. Its predominance in Western theatre is in a decline.

Signs and symbols

The use of signs and symbols to represent objects is a part of ordinary life, as well as a theatrical device. To take another example from one of Shakespeare's characters, in *Two Gentlemen of Verona* a servant described leaving home, and to make his account more vivid, used everyday objects to explain himself. The effect was comical:

> This shoe is my father: no, this left shoe is my father: no, no, this left shoe is my mother: nay, that cannot be so neither: yes, it is so, it is so, it hath the worser sole. This shoe, with the hole in it, is my mother, and this my father; a vengeance on't! there 'tis; now, sir, this staff is my sister, for, look you, she is as white as a lily, and as small as a wand: this hat is Nan, our maid: I am the dog: no, the dog is himself, and I am the dog, – Oh! the dog is me, and I am myself; ay, so, so.
>
> (Act II, Scene ii, l. 14)

This is what anyone does when trying to explain a situation or a position to someone else. If giving directions while sitting at the breakfast-table, you will naturally use the cups and plates to represent the landmarks. Children learn to do this very early in life, using whatever comes to hand, to be part of their make-believe games. 'This is my baby', a child may say, tenderly cradling a piece of wood or cloth. Only later, when he/she has seen a real doll, will the child crave for the more realistic representation. The facility to believe in a representative object does not depend on the object being an exact replica of the real thing. While Western realism developed the making of a replica into a highly sophisticated art, Eastern tradition instead made an art of the symbolic substitute.

The earliest country to develop this method of scenic art

was China. Theatre tradition there went back as far as 1000 BCE. Entertainments continued throughout the centuries, with a great flowering during the Yuan dynasty (1279–1368), and a continuous development, culminating in the dominance of Peking Opera as the classical form since the mid-nineteenth century. The conventions of the Peking Opera derived from these earlier periods. They were striking in their visual simplicity. Often only a light wooden table and some chairs stood on the stage. These permanent properties were used to symbolise whatever setting was needed – a law court, a banqueting hall or other interior scene. They were swiftly arranged in a prescribed manner by the property man and his assistants, who remained in full view all the time. The chairs and table represented any number of objects and settings – a wall (two chairs back to back), a mountain (chairs piled on top of each other), a bridge (chairs with backs to the end of the table), a loom, prison gates, the edge of a well, a precipice and so forth. Many other simple properties were used, stimulating the spectators' interest, but leaving much to their imaginations. Weapons were made of bamboo, wood or rattan, for skilful manipulation. Other examples of properties included: a wooden board painted with wavy lines to indicate clouds; a lantern on poles to indicate darkness; two yellow flags with wheels to indicate a chariot; black silk streamers to indicate the wind or a storm; a piece of gauze held above the head to indicate that the actor was dreaming; a paddle wrapped in a garment to indicate a corpse. The skill with which the actor transformed these objects created enjoyment and admiration, locking the spectators into the dramatic situation. In this tradition, still practised in the Chinese theatre, the actors revel in their own skill at evoking scenes, creating through mime the exact motion of a boat, for example, with two actors bobbing up and down in rhythm. In a famous comic scene, a thief is discovered breaking into a dark room. The occupant tries to catch the thief, the thief tries to escape. It is all supposed to be happening in the dark, but the scene is played in full light. The spectators roar with laughter as the actors narrowly miss each other, groping in the 'dark'.

The *Noh* plays, too, are performed against a permanent screen, without additional scenery. When objects are needed,

Chinese actor holds a whip to represent a horse

whether a tree or a door or an animal, the actor simply manipulates his fan to indicate it. No trickery is used. Everyone knows it is a fan, and this shared knowledge adds to the enjoyment and appreciation of the actors' skill. Just as it takes years of training for a *Noh* actor to learn the uses of the mask, so too with the fan, which must represent all the things with which the character comes in contact.

The *Kabuki* theatre has developed a more lavish style of scenery and properties which mix decorative and realistic. Simplified replicas are used, to cover a large number of settings. A house, in *Kabuki* theatre, has paper doors to form the walls, mats on a raised platform for the floor, a curtained entrance way and a lattice gate. A black cyclorama indicates that the scene takes place at night. Brilliantly coloured curtains feature prominently. Properties are carried with great style, to enhance the total effect of the actor's appearance, rather than for practical purposes.

Both kinds of scenery described so far, the realistic and the symbolic, represent one location at a time. But another convention has been used where the stage represents more than one scene simultaneously.

Multiple staging

The first notable use of multiple staging was in the Middle Ages in Europe, between the classical period and the Renaissance. As we have seen, the mystery plays were performed on pageant wagons, or mansions. These could be regarded as single stages for the performance of an individual play. But when gathered round the whole stage area, whether it was market-place or cathedral steps, they functioned rather as scenic units, each of which provided the visual focus at different times. The central part of the stage area, called in Latin the *platea*, or place, was a kind of common territory. Actors could 'journey' from one mansion to another. Relative distance, so important in perspective scenery, was irrelevant to medieval drama. Actors waiting for their scene sat in their own mansions, able to observe the drama, visible to the audience, but ignored by them. When the professional players rose to prominence in the sixteenth century, they took over the same conventions, though less lavishly, since they had to supply all their scenery, not just one mansion. So they gathered a collection of stock units – a grassy bank, an arbour, a castle turret, a throne of state and so on – to define different locations on the single stage. When they were invited to perform at Court, the budget was bigger and more lavish units could be provided.

The playwrights of Shakespeare's time drew on both European scenic conventions, sometimes setting their scenes in one location which could be created by a permanent set, sometimes switching rapidly from one location to another, requiring the audience to switch their attention too, with the help of a mansion or scenic unit, or an explanatory line such as: 'So this is the Forest of Arden', from *As You Like It*.

We see then that the scene can be set through words, gestures, objects that are realistic or symbolic, scenic illusion and decoration. The next questions to address are these: what happens *between* the scenes? how is the scenery to be changed? The conventions established between actors and spectators are most delicately balanced during those moments when, temporarily, the illusion is broken.

The changing of scenes

In those traditions which rely most on the actor, changes of scene can be instantaneous. In Shakespeare's theatre, characters exited, new ones entered. By their speech you learnt quickly where they were, though often it was sufficient to see who they were and hear what they were saying. The first editions of Shakespeare's texts gave few stage directions. In editions printed afterwards, the stage directions often said something vague like 'Another part of the forest', because the exact location was not important.

In classical Chinese theatre, too, the actors' narrative plays an important part, holding the action together. As we have seen, they create the scenery through their use of simple objects. Little physical scene-changing is necessary. Where it is needed, stage-hands enter, to bring in or remove the objects, and then the play proceeds. Probably the same thing happened within the medieval convention. Since little was made of the difference between actors and spectators, it was unlikely to have troubled anyone if pauses occurred during which scenery was moved about, ready for the next scene.

In other traditions also, the changing of scenes has been minimal. Stage décor has sometimes developed as part of theatre architecture, providing a permanent background for the plays to be presented, using the basic materials of the building, such as stone or wood. Examples of such permanent settings include:

(1) Greek and Roman stone theatres, with their proscenium stone screens and doorways. Additional scenic units were added.
(2) Indian theatres, decorated with elaborate carvings.
(3) Chinese theatre, performed against a smooth plain wall in which two doors are placed.
(4) The wooden O of Shakespeare's time, with its façade of balconies and doorways. Scenic units were added where needed, in the medieval tradition.
(5) *Noh* theatre, with a permanent background of a pine tree.

(6) Théâtre du Vieux Colombier in Paris. An early twentieth-century example of a theatre designed with a permanent setting.
(7) Festival Theatre, Stratford, Ontario. A mid-twentieth-century example.

One of the advantages of using a multipurpose setting is that the audience's mind can be switched to another location even within the same scene. In Greek tragedy, the messenger character often painted a vivid word picture of an offstage scene, a picture which the audience could superimpose on the undistracting scene presented before their eyes. Yet medieval audiences seem to have been able to ignore that kind of distraction, or to see it in the context of *all* the scenes. However, from the time of the Renaissance, a convention began to be established in which one scene at a time was set before the spectators, each one providing a complete visual experience. In such a convention the scenery is changed from scene to scene.

Movable scenery

Scenery that is brought on and off the stage must be developed to fit the conditions of the performance. Much depends on the kind of theatre it is to be used in. A lot depends on economics too. Can the production have scenery specially created for it, or must it be mounted using only what is available? Although technological changes have affected the development of scenery, often other factors have had an even greater influence.

One of the oldest forms of movable scenery was used in the Greek theatres, and is still a useful and adaptable method. A framework was made in the shape of a triangular pillar – rather like a giant Toblerone chocolate bar. When covered with fabric, each of the three facets of these *periaktoi*, as they were called, was painted and could be turned either towards or away from the audience. For example, one side might be painted to suggest landscape, another like a pillar. A number of them placed together would considerably alter the appearance of the stage. It was a version of this classical method that inspired Serlio to create the perspective series of screens for the Renaissance theatre. But his search to create perspective made him alter their shape to angle wings, and fix their position.

Two factors in the European quest for realism affected the construction of scenery importantly. One, already mentioned, was the need to create a unified stage picture in perspective. This necessitated finding ways of fixing the position of scenery precisely. Various methods for moving and fixing wings and screens were explored, including the provision of grooves on the stage floor, along which pieces of scenery could be slid on and off. Groove and shutter scenery can still be seen in well-preserved European theatres.

The other factor was the convention of changing the scenery without the stage-hands being visible. As Renaissance scenery developed in complexity and ingenuity, the element of wonder and delight was keenly sought. It became a source of pride to create complicated effects and scene changes as if by magic. A Renaissance guide to scene construction contained long instructions for transforming the scene before the spectators' eyes without any stage-hands being visible. As theatre machinery increased in complexity, it became possible to store scenery above the stage. This area became known as the flies, because a system of pulleys and ropes, with sandbags as counterweights, could be used to fly the scenery in and out of the stage. Large numbers of unseen stage-hands were needed. Theatres in nineteenth-century industrial cities thrived on the cheap labour they could get. Often stage-hands were recruited from the navy, since the setting up of scenery was not unlike the rigging of sails on a ship. A theatrical superstition against whistling in the theatre is said to derive from this custom of using navvies, for whom various kinds of whistle were a signal to let go of a rope. If someone whistled at the wrong moment, they might end up with a sandbag or a scene flat on their head.

As changes grew complicated, the separation between stage and auditorium was useful, because a curtain could be lowered. Like the mask worn by an actor, a curtain can serve the double function of concealing and revealing. Another word for theatre curtains is tabs, short for tableaux, or pictures, which can be painted on them. If a theatre is equipped with enough rails, it can provide a number of painted or decorated tabs which serve as background to a scene. Other curtains can be used to conceal the offstage areas (such curtains are sometimes called legs), or the lighting equipment above the stage (such curtains are called borders). In a proscenium theatre, the front curtain that conceals the stage from the audience is very evocative. Often made of rich fabric such as red velvet, it sets the mood for a pleasurable occasion. From the moment when it rises, revealing the stage for the first time, to the very end, when it falls for the last time, cutting short the action and separating the actors, the audience is caught up in the enjoyment of a make-believe world. So evocative is this curtain, that the very word conjures up the magic of theatre for many people in the English-speaking world. Titles of books about theatre include *Curtain Up* and *Ring Up The Curtain!* The word 'Curtains!' is sometimes used as slang for the end of something, even the death of someone. The question, 'What time is the curtain?' means when does the play begin or end.

The transformation from one scene to another is an important part of the enjoyment of spectacular scenery. In the Victorian theatre a mountain scene might be changed to a gorgeous palace before your very eyes, or a whole city might pass before your gaze. When such excitement was a distraction, or the expense was too great, curtains were used to conceal the scene-change. Either a relatively unimportant scene could be played in front of the tabs that concealed the back half of the stage, in which case various thumps and rumblings would be heard; or else the front curtain was lowered and an interval, sometimes monotonously long, occurred.

Curtains and spectacular transformations were also important in the *Kabuki* theatre, with greater emphasis on decoration than on authentic realism. In the search for new ways of delighting the eye, the Eastern and European traditions had developed with different emphases between the fifteenth and nineteenth centuries, the one seeking decorative costumes against a comparatively simple background, together with grace of movement and gesture by the actors, while the other created worlds within worlds, to delight the spectators and give them the childlike enjoyment of make-believe.

In the European style, developing technology played an important part. Until the twentieth century, the materials for scenery did not vary much. Wood, fabric, paint and paper were the main materials, with metals used either decoratively or as part of the support structure. However, the invention of lightweight alloys like aluminium, and of synthetics like fibreglass, polystyrene and powerful adhesives, has greatly increased the useful stock in a scene shop. New kinds of machinery, too, have been quickly adapted for theatrical use. Improved engineering made it possible, by the twentieth century, to move large scenic units on and off and around the stage. These units or wagons are aptly named, since they are like mobile medieval mansions in effect. They brought a return to three-dimensional scenery after centuries in which the two-dimensional had dominated. The *Kabuki* theatre was the first to develop a revolving stage, which brings different scenic units into view as it rotates. But the biggest technological development for scenic art was the development of electric lighting.

Modern lighting in the theatre

Gas lighting was introduced in European theatres in the early nineteenth century, quickly followed by limelight, a dazzling light made by heating quicklime (or calcium oxide) to incandescence. Soon the very phrase 'in the limelight', came to be linked with stardom. Electric lighting was introduced in the late nineteenth century, making illumination both efficient and effective. Before that, candles and oil-lamps had been used in many ingenious ways, to illuminate and to create special effects in the theatre.

Just as important as providing light, was creating shade and darkness where and when needed. Until lighting was controllable, area by area, the actors and the spectators had both been lit. But in the nineteenth century the auditorium was darkened, increasing the vividness of the stage action, allowing the spectators almost to forget their own existence. Scenes could be ended by a black-out, instead of by lowering the curtain. Very useful for a quick ending, such as is needed for a comic sketch with a punchline, or a moment of dramatic suspense. Also, certain areas of the stage could be darkened when not needed. This meant that the multiple scenes used in the medieval tradition could be reintroduced without upsetting the conventions of realism. Gradually, the quality of the lighting began to be incorporated into the whole visual scheme of the production. Previously, colour and texture had been indicated mainly through skilful painting. Special effects, through using fire, moving lights or beams filtered through silk, had been hampered by the difficulty of controlling naked flames (though firework displays had played their part in theatre). Now such effects were technically easier to achieve. Also, since light and shade could be controlled, the shape and mass of scenic units became more significant. Three-dimensional, architectural scenery offered scope for creating very different effects with one set. One early twentieth-century director used a flight of stairs for his set, recalling the simplicity of classical theatres.

Scenic art was not divorced from the other visual arts. In Europe, during the early years of the twentieth century, new developments in painting and sculpture were paralleled in the theatre. Realism ceased to be the only important scenic style. The impressionistic quality of light, the increased interest in psychology, in dreams and the unconscious, made the creation of mood, atmosphere and underlying meaning as important as a representation of the environment. At the same time, the separation of the two main theatrical traditions, European and Asian, now began to be bridged. Asian theatres began to introduce more realism, sometimes retaining their older traditions alongside the European style, while Western theatres introduced decorative and symbolic scenery and props. The role of the stage designer became increasingly important in stimulating and controlling the spectators' visual experience.

Stage design in the modern world

We have seen that in primitive theatre the roles of playwright and performer may overlap. Similarly the function of stage design has not always been distinguished from other functions of theatre. If a strong visual convention exists, playwright, actors and/or stage-manager can decide on the scenery and props, and arrange them appropriately. For plays with elaborate settings, the stage-manager's role increases in complexity. He/she needs a large team to handle the different part of the work – a property master/mistress, a wardrobe master/mistress, stage-hands and assistants – but still the overall design may not need supervision. The stage designer makes his/her appearance when the scenic effect is recognised as a creative and innovative part of the whole production. This occurred in Renaissance theatre, when named designers, such as the Italian Nicolo Sabbatini (1574–1654), and Inigo Jones in England (1573–1652), began to influence the theatre. Over the following centuries, many individual scenic artists appeared, achieving spectacular effects through their designs, and introducing innovations which influenced the development of stage design. They included the Bibiena family in eighteenth-century Italy, and Philippe de Loutherbourg, who worked in France and Italy, then settled in England in 1771 and worked for the actor/manager David Garrick.

Throughout the nineteenth century, the art of scene design and scene painting continued to develop in Europe. Towards the end of the century, and in the early twentieth century, revolutionary ideas about art and society began to hum, a prelude to many innovations in stage design. Nowhere was this revolution more exciting than in Russia. Poised as it was between the Western and Eastern parts of the world, and on the brink of social revolution, Russia nurtured a number of brilliant stage designers whose explosive influence is still felt. Germany and Central Europe also provided a seedbed where new ideas were germinated. The period from 1890 to 1930 was as fruitful in Central European theatre, including Russian, as the Renaissance had been in Western Europe. Social, economic and cultural ferment, the First World War and the Bolshevik Revolution, the increase in world communications, all combined to create a cauldron in which new and traditional kinds of theatre were mixed together in deliberately experimental work.

Here follow a few examples of these innovative designers. There was Adolphe Appia (1862–1928), a Swiss designer inspired and influenced by Richard Wagner's ideas. He introduced a more three-dimensional style of design and exploited the new potential of stage lighting to mould shapes through the creation of light and shade. Another was Edward Gordon Craig (1872–1906), an English designer whose work did not fit well into the theatre of his own culture, dominated by the actor and the spoken word. His idea of theatre was based on visual images. He imagined a theatre with no play, no plot, but correlated movements of sound, light and movement, all designed by one person, Sergei Diaghilev (1872–1929) was not a designer himself, but an impresario who developed the Russian ballet and brought it to Europe and other parts of the world. He encouraged stage design that was inventive, often fantastic, and brilliantly decorative, using artists such as Alexandre Benoit (1870–1960), Léon Bakst (1866–1924), and Pablo Picasso (1881–1973). Also from Russia was Vsevolid Meyerhold (1874–1943), the leader of avant-garde theatre in Soviet Russia during the 1920s. He broke down many of the barriers between actor and audience which had grown up in Western theatre, creating theatre that was a revelry of light, colour and movement. He moved the theatre away from realism, using, among other styles, constructivism, which used the industrialised, urban world of wheels, machines, scaffolding and so on to create abstract but functional setting. As a last example, there is Erwin Piscator (1893–1966), a German director who created new forms of political theatre. He created multistage, multimedia productions, using film, slides, placards and music-hall styles to create *agitprop* theatre that was immediately relevant.

In many parts of the world, spectators are now adaptable to several kinds of scenic convention, and even to a mixture of conventions in one production. There are no hard and fast rules about what is acceptable as an imitation of the characters' surroundings. The stage may be seen simultaneously as the platform where the actors perform; an unnamed location where the action occurs; and/or one or more specific locations. The scenery may provide a functional background or construction, in front of which, or on which, the performance occurs; the illusion of a fictional place; and/or an evocation of mood, atmosphere and meaning.

Stage properties, too, are created through a number of different conventions. Let us take, as an example, something often needed in representations of human activity, the horse.

In Chinese theatre, a whip held in the hand conventionally suggested that the actor was riding. In *Kabuki* theatre, a horse is represented by a wooden scaffold. It is of the right size and has four legs, but the resemblance to a real horse ends there. The actor's skill transforms it into a horse. The British representation of horses in the theatre has been rather different. Here too, in folk tradition, a wood object was used, a hobby horse. But with the quest for realism, such a device began to seem comical on stage. Shakespeare encouraged his audience to see horses by the use of language and thought:

> Think, when we talk of horses, that you see them
> Printing their proud hooves i'the receiving earth.
> (*Henry V*, Act i, Scene i, l. 26)

By the nineteenth century there were some bold actors who would bring a real horse upon the stage, despite the obvious difficulties it created (especially if the horse was taken short in the middle of the performance). There is also a comic tradition still used in Christmas pantomimes, where two actors play the horse. Perhaps the most unrewarding part in the British actor's repertoire is to be the back legs of the horse. Where the *Kabuki* actor could use an unrealistic toy, and be taken seriously, for the British actor a horse on stage was either real, or part of a comic turn. At last, in 1973, a new convention was established in a play called *Equus*, by Peter Shaffer, in which, for the first time, British actors represented the dignity of the horse, wearing wire-frame head-pieces and hooves. They did not resemble the *Kabuki* horse, but the same kind of convention was established, with an impression of a horse being skilfully created on stage.

Nowhere more than in the field of scenic effect do we see the huge number of choices open to the modern designer, who can choose between many conventions, and offer a simple or elaborate set. Spectators quickly learn to accept realistic, decorative or symbolic scenery; to be caught up in a convincing illusion for up to about two hours without a break, or to be aware of the elements of theatre being put together piece by piece. The delicate balance between involvement and detachment may alter from play to play, production to production. But although the possibility of using a number of scenic conventions is firmly established, the question of how much emphasis the scenic effect should have, is still debatable.

Word versus spectacle

During the rustics' play in *A Midsummer Night's Dream*, Shakespeare raised an easy laugh when the character of Starveling announced to the audience:

> All that I have to say, is to tell you, that the lanthorn is the moon, I the man i'the moon, this thorn-bush my thorn-bush, and this dog my dog.
>
> (Act v, Scene i, l. 247)

One reason these lines were comical was that the words were unnecessary, because Starveling's appearance, with the appropriate props, told all. When word and visual image duplicate, they do not always enrich each other, but render one superfluous and sometimes ridiculous. Battle has often been waged over whether the actor or the scenery is most important. One of Shakespeare's contemporaries, the playwright Ben Jonson, wrote contemptuously of the first great English scene designer, Inigo Jones, whose elaborate scenic effects rendered his poetry redundant. The fact is that a real image is often at odds with a mental image conjured up by word or gesture. Sometimes actors and playwrights are wearied by the technical complexities of scenic effects, knowing that the power of the imagination to build scenery can be greater than the most lavish set. But the creation of spectacle has its own allure. So much so, that the scenic designer may be tempted to do away with actors altogether, as Edward Gordon Craig did when he wrote of a theatre for *Übermarionetten*, or giant puppets.

So, in examining scenic effect, we discover a contradiction. On the one hand, scenery is expendable: the basics of theatre are actors, audience, a time and place, a drama to be performed. On the other hand, scenic art, the invention and physical creation of an imagined place, has a powerful fascination. It is as if Man had taken on the power of a god, able to create and destroy a world at will. In Shakespeare's *The Tempest*, this parallel is clearly drawn. The magician

Prospero arranges a masque, or lavish visual entertainment. As he brings it to an end, he compares its vanishing with the end of the world:

> like the baseless fabric of this vision,
> The cloud-capp'd towers, the gorgeous palaces,
> The solemn temples, the great globe itself,
> Yea, all which it inherit, shall dissolve,
> And like this insubstantial pageant faded,
> Leave not a rack behind.
>
> (Act IV, Scene i, l. 151)

The created world is like a great theatre, where gods or nature are the director, designer and playwright. Conversely, theatre is an image of the created world. Perhaps if we see, enjoy and understand the image, we see, enjoy and understand the world more easily.

8

Dance, music and sound

A YOUNG woman dying of consumption – tuberculosis – sings a four-minute aria that rings through a large opera house; a jilted princess shows her anger by standing on tiptoe on one leg and rotating herself thirty-two times; all the passers-by in a city street suddenly join together, dancing and singing in co-ordinating steps and tunes. All these moments can seem ludicrously unnatural for audiences who do not have experience of musical theatre, or who do not much like it. Yet the human urge to express feelings, particularly highly-charged feelings, in song and dance, is as old as spoken language itself, if not older. Spoken language is a means of communicating rational ideas, though poetic language communicates more than that. But before words came, there was pure utterance – a baby's cry, a laugh, a gurgle, a cooing. Before the flow of sentences, or the sequence of question followed by answer, there was the rhythm of the beating heart, of breathing, of rocking. Before language found precise ways of defining pleasure and pain, voices and bodies expressed them anyway, with leaping, shouting, growling, stamping, yodelling and a myriad other forms of movement and utterance. And from the birth of mankind, there were the sounds and movements of the natural world to hear and imitate, from the sighing of the wind in swaying trees, to the steady footfall of the hunted beast. Weaving movement and utterance into patterns, creating instruments to enlarge the repertoire of sounds, men and women invented dance and music, and used them to increase the effectiveness of their story-telling and dramas.

Together, dance, music, story-telling and dramatisation make up the performing arts. Traditions in different countries have varied in the ways these strands of performance have been combined or separated. Neither is it always easy to discover the ways, because written records and still pictures are a fragmentary way of recalling a performance. Greek tragedies, for example, contained much singing and dancing by the Chorus, but surviving scripts only tell us the words of the drama. But where tradition is continuous, folk dances and songs in many parts of the world have been handed down without being written down until recent history. While musical notation is many centuries old, dance notation is a comparatively modern skill.

European opera and ballet

Within the limitations set by these restrictions on knowledge, we can distinguish a European development from the time of the Renaissance, which, yet again, differed considerably from other traditions. In Asian and African theatre, music and dance remained fully integrated into the dramatic performance, while in Europe they branched out into different forms of the theatrical art. It is not appropriate, in this book, to compare or analyse the Western and Eastern styles of music and dance. They differed considerably in themselves. It is still difficult for many people to attune to the difference in sound. African styles of music and dance have more quickly been integrated into Western culture, adapting into jazz, rock'n'roll and other modern styles, which helped to restore a vital link between music and dance which had become somewhat separated in the highest forms of Western art.

In Europe two distinct forms of musical theatre emerged – opera and ballet. Both were sophisticated forms of entertainment, developed in cities and courts from the sixteenth century onward. Opera first developed in Italy, and ballet in France, the languages of both arts still being the main source of terminology. In the eighteenth century, Germany and Austria also excelled in opera, through the genius of Mozart and others, and in the nineteenth century Russia, under strong French cultural influence, brought the art of classical ballet to its highest level. Both these forms of musical drama spread throughout Europe, and were taken to other parts of the world, together with the spoken drama, as part of colonial development. Specialisation was paramount.

The physical exertions of operatic singing were entirely different from those of classical ballet. Both required a high degree of technical expertise, which often predominated over the drama. Nevertheless, both developed as powerful forms of theatrical expression.

In opera, the strength and endurance of the voice was linked with human struggle, especially, in the nineteenth century, the struggle of the individual over oppressive forces. The operatic voice, soaring above a full orchestra, seemed the appropriate medium for the romantic urge to fulfil one's destiny over all odds. Let us examine one example.

Fidelio, composed by Ludwig van Beethoven with libretto by J. Sonnleithner (1805)
The great German composer wrote only one opera. Classical music, by his time, had developed its own dramatic form, the symphony, in which different parts of the orchestra took up and developed a kind of abstract story-line, which eventually resolved at the end of a movement. A whole symphony, consisting of about four movements was something like a *Noh* programme of plays, presenting sections of different moods which led to a culminating resolution at the end. For Beethoven, to turn to the stage was to make a conscious choice to create human drama through music. This was partly in homage to his great predecessor, Mozart, partly from an awareness of the human drama being played out around him. He saw in opera the opportunity to express the revolutionary cry for *Freedom!* that was echoing through nineteenth-century Europe, as different groups and nations sought liberation from some form of tyranny.

Fidelio is the story of the overthrow of a tyrant, focusing on a prisoner who has been shut up for many years, reminiscent of Charles Dickens's *A Tale of Two Cities*. The woman who loved him disguised herself as a man to come and rescue him. Opera had often used the tradition of girl-dressed-as-boy, not as in Shakespeare's time, so that a boy could more easily play it, but rather as a breeches part, with a woman playing a man, so that the power and flexibility of a woman's voice could be exploited in the more active role a man might play in the drama. Here, the change of clothes is part of the story. Later, Richard Strauss would simply cast his hero as a soprano, in *Der Rosenkavalier*, as Mozart had the young boy Cherubino in his *The Marriage of Figaro*.

Beethoven used his music to propel the revolutionary story towards its climax. Following the form of Mozartian opera the dialogue is carried through *recitativo*, the most informal vocal writing in classical opera, catching the rhythm and nuances of speech, but heightening the drama with music. Then, at crucial moments of tension and drama, the action is suspended for an aria, a powerful vocal exploration of the character's feelings, leading him or her forward to the next action, whether it is Fidelio's determination to free her lover, or the lover's acceptance of his own anguish and hopelessness in prison. The musical form also allows for another kind of exploration which goes further into the characters' minds than normal dialogue could take them. That is in a duet, trio, or ensemble, in which the action is again suspended, while two or more characters express their differing reactions to the same situation.

Another dramatic vocal method, used most effectively in *Fidelio*, was the chorus, which allowed the full company on stage to express the united emotion of a whole community. Nineteenth-century Europe was becoming conscious of the masses, the vast numbers that made up the populations, especially in the cities. It was perhaps for this reason that grand opera reached its height at this time. The almost superhuman voices of the trained singers, and the large choruses which could be amassed on stage, were the only adequate expression of the revolutionary fervour behind many social and national movements of the time. Thus, the climax of *Fidelio* is the Prisoners' Chorus, sung as the wretched people emerge into the light from the darkness and degradation in which they have long been shut. The chorus symbolises universal liberation.

In ballet too, physical strength and endurance expressed human struggle. Here though, it was linked with vulnerability. Where opera exploited the power of human passions, romantic ballet depicted lyricism, grace and apparent fragility, yet required great physical strength and stamina. Often the art was to disguise the discipline and physical exertion required.

Swan Lake (Lac des Cygnes), choreographed by Léon Petipa to music by Piotr Ilich Tchaikovsky (1895)
This is perhaps the most famous of romantic ballets. It tells the story of Odette, a princess transformed by an enchanter into a swan by day. The spell can be broken only if someone loves her who has sworn love to no one else. Prince Siegfried falls in love with her, but at the Ball where he is supposed to choose his bride, the enchanter brings his daughter Odile, resembling Odette. The Prince declares his love for her, failing to see a vision of Odette until too late. Heartbroken, Siegfried and Odette drown themselves in the swan lake. Their sacrifice breaks the spell and the enchanter dies. Beyond death, the couple journey towards eternal happiness.

This romance, with its evil forces, its test of love and its final apotheosis, requires the other-worldly quality of lyrical dance. Yet the ballet also appeals to those who admire technical expertise and feats of physical skill. The leading ballerina dances the demanding double role of Odette/Odile and dominates the work. The story is carried through mime, but relationships and feelings are conveyed through solos, *pas de deux* (dances for two), dances for small groups, and for a *corps de ballet*, a dancing chorus.

The basis of classical ballet movement was elevation. The dancer leapt or rose to express emotion, leaving the earth behind and giving an impression of weightlessness. The ballerina was often on points, in blocked shoes that hardly touched the ground at all. The body could seem to fly, to float, to sway like a reed, ripple like a wave. Ballet often exploited its lack of speech, showing the anguish of dumb suffering in Odette, the swan-maiden, and in the heroine of *Giselle*, who went mad. The great Russian ballerina, Anna Pavlova, also danced *The Dying Swan* and another famous bird ballet was *The Firebird*. Other ballets showed ethereal characters like sylphs, *Les Sylphides* and *La Sylphide*, a water nymph, *Ondine*, or a flower spirit, *Le Spectre de la Rose*. Modern dance and ballet in the twentieth century introduced earthier movements, but classical ballet still remained popular and spread to other countries. Its characteristic message was that love, which might seem too weak and fragile to survive, could nevertheless conquer evil through its powers of endurance.

In opera and ballet, the highest achievements were when the music, the technique, the décor and the dramatic expression were integrated. This was rarely achieved, because the specialisation of skills meant that a collective spirit was hard to sustain. Composer, librettist or choreographer, designer, voice or dance teacher, and performer, might all regard themselves as complete artists, and quarrel for pre-eminence. The idea of a prima donna, a leading lady whose tempers and whims dominated a production, first grew up in eighteenth-century Italian opera. The term can equally be applied to men. Sergei Diaghilev, the great autocratic Russian impresario, achieved great success for his company because he had the power to exploit many individual talents in the creation of a single piece of theatre.

Incidental music

As well as these specialised forms of musical theatre, music and dance remained a part of European spoken drama, but it was incidental, that is, reserved for intervals, interludes, special effects or special items on the programme. Music and dance were important in the plays of Shakespeare, for example. Great composers have written music for his play, including Felix Mendelssohn, whose music for *A Midsummer Night's Dream* is famous. Similarly, Edvard Grieg's music for Ibsen's *Peer Gynt* is a popular piece of classical music. Many different kinds of drama-with-music evolved in European theatre, including melodrama and operetta in the nineteenth century. Melodrama, where music was played under the action, to underline the drama as in film and television drama, was particularly important in England, where strict laws forbade the performance of spoken drama in all but two theatres in the capital. Operetta was a light-hearted or sentimental drama, enhanced by much music and dancing. It was particularly developed in Vienna, by such composers as Johann Strauss and family, and had an influence on the musical comedies of the twentieth century. In vaudeville and music-hall, recitations and comic or sentimental sketches alternated with music, acrobatics and other items, to create a variety programme.

Sound effects

Parallel to the different traditions in scenic effects, sound effects have been largely dominated, in the Western theatre, by the attempt to create an acceptable imitation of real sound, while in Eastern traditions sounds have often been created by on-stage musicians, to symbolise the real effect. In Shakespeare's time, plays demanded little else than alarums and excursions, that is, the sounds appropriate to an off-stage battle, plus fanfares and other ceremonial music. Storms also played their part, for example in *King Lear*. Later, as scenic realism developed, it became more important to suggest the existence of an off-stage world as convincing as the one on-stage. Simulation techniques were invented and passed on through generations of stage managers, including the clapping together of coconut shells for the sound of horses' hooves, the trickle of dried peas across a drum skin for the sound of a wave breaking on the shore, and the shaking of a metal sheet for the rumble of thunder. There was a temptation, in the heyday of realistic theatre, to create continuous background noise. The playwright Chekhov lamented much over the interminable sound of birdsong which the director Stanislavsky thought fit to add to one of his productions.

The invention of sound reproduction systems revolutionised Western theatre as much as electric lighting did. Incidental music, off-stage sounds could all be recorded, often with exciting stereophonic effects. A train, for example, could be heard proceeding from one part of the theatre to another, or cheering voices could be heard through the auditorium, giving the audience an extra participatory thrill.

Dance-drama and music outside Europe

One skill that got lost in Western theatre was the human power of imitating non-human sounds. Often a part of the story-teller's art, it remained an art among forest people in Africa, for example, paralleling the art of mime, and retaining the centrality of the actor in creating the environment for the drama.

All the major Asian forms of theatre unified music, words and gestures. This integration, as much as the symbolic and decorative scenic conventions, encouraged the development of non-realistic theatre. In particular, dance and drama were not separated, musical accompaniment marked the establishment of mood and emotion, speech and singing often merged into one form of heightened vocal delivery.

In India, drama developed in close association with temple dancing. The *Kathakali* dancers, whose art is most directly descended from the early theatre tradition, perform almost entirely in dance and mime, delivering the equivalent of monologues and conducting elaborate dialogues in movement. Narrators sing the story in a forceful style, to the accompaniment of percussion instruments. The traditions of theatre in Bali, Thailand, Cambodia and Burma have many similarities. Balinese dance-drama is the best known to the rest of the world. Performed by the community, it remains close to the heart of village culture.

One famous Balinese dance is the *Barong play*. The Barong is a kind of dragon, performed by two men (like the British pantomime horse), who has a fight with a witch, Rangda. When Barong is defeated, the villagers attack Rangda, but their daggers are turned magically upon themselves. The performers, in a trance-like state, are apparently unharmed by their own daggers. For Westerners this magical element seems unbelievable. But for the Balinese, the intensity of the dance is closely linked with religious fervour; the state of ecstasy they reach seems natural.

In another form of Balinese dance, *legong*, troupes of young girls, up to about fifteen years old, are trained for periods of six months. Three dancers perform, moving with astonishing vigour through long passages of choreography, apparently without fatigue. One dance is about the arrogant King Lasem, who stole Princess Rangkesvari when she rejected his suit. She refused to submit and he threatened to kill her father in battle. But as he set off, a black bird flew down in front of him, an unlucky omen, and he himself was killed. The climax of the dance is when the bird approaches the king, advancing and retreating, fluttering her wings and beating the earth. A crescendo of intense movement and sound is reached. Then suddenly the dancers arrive at the temple steps and are transformed back into being simple village girls.

Legong dancer of Bali

In China and Japan, music is also integral to the traditional theatre. Peking Opera is totally unlike Western opera. The singing is not continuous, but it is a dominant part of the performance. In earlier periods in China, drama was more literary, but in this form, which reached its climax in the nineteenth century, acting, singing and orchestral accompaniment carry the main action. The orchestra includes several percussive instruments, such as gongs, cymbals, drums and clappers, as well as some string instruments and woodwind. They perform in full view of the audience, introducing, accompanying and providing interludes or bridge passages between song and action. Programmes of Peking Opera are often long and varied. The enjoyment does not depend on a continuous dramatic development, but on a display of skill and variety. The songs are often familiar in musical content, as are the scenic conventions and the words and gestures used by the actors. This famous popular tradition of theatre is in contrast, not only to Western theatre, but to other elitist, intellectual forms of theatre, such as *Noh*. The atmosphere is casual, more reminiscent of a sports event than a sophisticated artistic event, and highly appreciated by its audience.

Music in *Noh* theatre intensifies the action. Two styles of singing are used. One is 'weak', more like declamation, the other is 'strong'. But neither style emphasises melody, requires a large vocal range, nor depends on richness of tone. The singing uses rhythm and intonation to concentrate meaning. The orchestra is in view, and consists mainly of drums and flute. To Western ears the sounds are weird and disjointed, with cries, growls and single notes punctuating the action. Dance, too, is integrated into acting and gesture. A *Noh* programme, consisting of several plays, has a clear progression. Each play consists of an introduction, *jo*, a development, *ha*, and climax, *kyu*. The pace increases from a deliberate, slow beginning to the strenuous, often agitated movements of a final dance. The programme follows the same progression: the first play is calm and dignified, in the middle come warrior plays and love plays, while the last plays may be of madness or demons. Thus, the tension increases as the performance develops. The dances echo this pattern, beginning with solemn, lengthy dances, *mai*, and moving on to vigorous, even wild dances, *hataraki*, which form the climax. Here the full intensity of the *Noh* performance is felt. It is an art best appreciated by the connoisseur, who does not judge by the quality of the dancer's technique, as in classical ballet, but by the ability of the actor to express with his whole body what one has called 'the torment, serene joy or bittersweet longing' felt by the character.

Though often in contrast to the contemplative form of *Noh*, *Kabuki* theatre too, uses musical accompaniment and dance, as well as acrobatics and other physical activity. The dancing enhances the performer's vivid and decorative display, characterised by dramatic poses and leaps which increase the tension and excitement of his performance.

In other parts of the world too, dance and music are integrated into the drama. Ritual drama in American Indian tribes is not separated from dance. In African tribal theatre, little distinction is made between verbal, musical and physical language. The forms merge as the performers adopt whichever mode is immediately appropriate to the atmosphere, emotion and meaning of the moment. The drum is essential, the rhythm and chanting of dancing and singing is deliberately infectious, uniting performers and spectators in a complete experience.

Music in the modern theatre

The essential elements in theatre are the time and space, the actors, the audience and the play. Scenery, music and dancing are not essential. When they are present, the event takes on a multimedia aspect, which can raise it to a higher level of celebration. If the aural and visual senses are bombarded with many experiences, no clear meaning may emerge. For ritual theatre in a close community, this does not matter, because the participants know beforehand the significance of the event. For some events, such as carnivals and happenings, the formless anarchic nature of the occasion is part of the attraction. But where theatrical art has been consciously innovative and inventive, discipline has been used, to combine the different theatrical media clearly and effectively. In the Eastern theatre, the scenic effect has usually been simple. The performers use music, speech and movement to symbolise the meaning of the drama they have evolved. In the European theatre, either spoken language or scenic effect has been dominant. Different branches of theatrical art have developed, using speech, dance or singing as the vehicle to express the drama.

In the late nineteenth century, the characteristic development of the Western and Eastern traditions began to change. One can see this change as the beginning of a world view of theatre. The interchange of cultures increased, and knowledge was revealed of the whole length and spread of human activity. In the West, a nostalgia was felt for the times when theatre had not been separated into specialisms, but was an integrated expression of the whole community. In Germany, the composer/dramatist Richard Wagner looked back to the great Theatre of Dionysos. (His counterparts in sport were looking back to the great Olympic games and dreamed up the idea of reviving them for the modern world.) Wagner's greatest work was a vast music/drama cycle called *Der Ring des Nibelungen*, in which he adapted some of the myths of northern Europe, drawing a parallel with modern civilisation. Determined to integrate all the elements of theatre, he supervised much of the scenic effect, as well as writing the music and the words. He coined the term *Gesamtkunstwerk*, which means a work of combined art, to describe what he was doing. He also had a theatre built to house his operas. With his *Gesamtkunstwerk* and the architecture of the theatre at Bayreuth, he hoped to restore a sense of communal celebration.

But in the next generation, the playwright Bertolt Brecht interpreted the combined arts of theatre differently. He criticised the Wagnerian theatre because it swept the audience/spectators into a world of mythical fantasies where they could forget the real world, and forget they were in a theatre. Brecht's most famous musical drama was a deliberate mockery of the Wagnerian style.

The Threepenny Opera (1928)
This was not a conventional opera along the Italian lines, but was based on an eighteenth-century English burlesque piece, *The Beggar's Opera*, in which thieves and common criminals aped the manners of gentlemen and fine ladies, including their elitist art, the opera. The overt meaning of the play could also be turned on its head. The play was a satire on the gentlemen of the time, specifically the politicians, showing them to be as liable to cheating, bribery and corruption as the common criminals. Brecht switched the story to American gangsterland, showing that capitalist businessmen were just as bad as criminals.

The Beggar's Opera had used popular tunes, changing the words so that the music was part of the burlesque. Songs and dances were not fully integrated into the story. This was an accurate imitation of English opera of the time, which resisted for many years the Italian tradition of telling the whole drama through continuous music. Brecht preferred this breaking-up of speech and music. While many operatic composers strove to create a seamless music/drama, he deliberately disrupted the continuity, in order to set off one element of theatre against another. He was just as enthusiastic as Wagner about using all the elements of theatre, but with several important differences which are worth pointing out.

Firstly, Brecht did not want theatre to be a special event, requiring special behaviour, but something that was part of ordinary experience, like going to a sporting event or a beer-cellar. In this, he was influenced by the Chinese theatre, where tea and food were served, and the audience chatted and joked while the play was going on. Secondly, Brecht wanted the mechanics of theatre to be visible, not hidden mysteriously behind curtains. Similarly, skills should not be specialised, requiring years of training cut off from ordinary life. Thirdly, he wanted the audience to notice the different elements of theatre, such as music or costume, and question their significance. Brecht wanted the audience conscious of alternative possibilities, not wrapped up in the performance, uncritical of its implications for them. This was what he called *Verfremdungseffekt* – alienation effect.

Contemporary with Brecht's work, a new form of musical theatre was developing which would meet some of his requirements – the American musical. The United States of America were the first European colonies to become politically independent, and the first to make their own contribution to Western theatre. The musical comedy, which developed during the first quarter of the twentieth century, was a new, highly self-conscious, but popular form of musical theatre, which soon spread to wider audiences. An early example is discussed below.

Show Boat, composed by Jerome Kern, words by Oscar Hammerstein (1927)
This was the first great American musical. Based on a novel, it told an American story, set around the Mississippi River, with one of the characters a poor and exhausted southern negro. The songs became famous in their own right, especially 'Can't Help Lovin' Dat Man' and 'Ol' Man River'. They also fitted into the story well.

The musical combined performing arts in a new way. New forms of dance were introduced into the theatre, like tap and modern, which were more earthy than ballet. Songs consisted of ballads, novelty numbers and ensembles, deriving from variety, vaudeville and music-hall entertainments. Audiences who found the conventions of opera and ballet artificial, and the atmosphere elitist, had no problem making the jump from realistic speech to song and dance which expressed the more heightened emotions. The musical drew on a universal desire to sing and dance, which classical opera and ballet had to some extent lost. The stories often reflected the optimism of white America, with its ideals of freedom, prosperity and success for the ordinary man. Thus a new myth, the American dream, was born, and celebrated through a new ritual, the Broadway musical. From *Chorus Line* to *Jesus Christ Superstar*, the 'musical' is now one of the most popular forms of theatrical entertainment, drawing its stories, music and choreography from many different traditions, performed in many parts of the world.

9
The performance

The role of the audience

However limited your experience of theatre you have probably been in the audience for at least one performance of a play. You may have been to dozens. In modern theatre, the role of the audience varies very widely, depending upon the expectations and experience of each individual, as well as on the nature of the production. For example, one person seeing an opera at Covent Garden may be impressed by the magnificence of décor and music, another embarrassed by the fact that one of the singers is overweight and unconvincing as a lover, while a third may criticise the technique of the performers, comparing them with others who have played the same role. Yet they are all members of the same audience. Because we sit quietly and listen in modern theatre, it is easy to forget that the role of the audience is not passive.

We have seen that ritual drama was often performed for a specific purpose. This purpose was shared by performers and actors: for instance, to honour the dead, to pray for prosperity, to celebrate triumphs, to educate members of the community, to share the values of the society. It should not be forgotten that all these purposes are still valid. The problem is that we do not always know in advance what purpose a particular play has. 'Going to the theatre' is usually a form of entertainment, but what does 'entertainment' mean? To entertain is to amuse, or to occupy the time agreeably. That is a very wide definition. People are 'entertained' by very different kinds of theatre. Sometimes the occasion of the play tells you something of its purpose. A school play, for example, is partly to celebrate the achievements of the performers, but theatre-in-education has a different purpose, to teach. A Christmas pantomime is a seasonal celebration, like a carnival, allowing some time for irreverent and irresponsible enjoyment.

If you know beforehand the type of play you are going to see, you may understand its purpose. A mystery, or detective play, for example, is a riddle which you can try to solve, while a thriller gives you the chance to experience danger in an enjoyable way (like riding on a roller coaster). But for many plays, both serious and comic, there are several purposes and some are only revealed as the play progresses. Sometimes you think you know the main purpose, and you judge accordingly, missing some other purpose you had not actually considered. For example, many people assume that a musical is a light-hearted celebration of love and success; but the musical *Sweeney Todd* explored a grim and macabre Victorian world, and was misunderstood by many. Often if you have studied the text of a play before seeing it, you assume you know the purpose of the production. But the actors, designer and director may have a different purpose in staging the play. Therefore the first task of the modern theatre audience is often to be open-minded, to enter the theatre ready to appreciate and respond to whatever the entertainment offers.

As you recognise the nature of a play or a production, or learn about it in advance from someone else, you begin to discover the specific tasks given to the audience. Sometimes the tasks relate to the meaning of the play. Are you being asked to judge? Are you being warned? Is your sympathy being demanded? Are you being invited to identify with one or more characters? Other tasks relate to the conventions of the theatre. Are you being asked to pretend the play world is real? Or that it symbolises something? Are you being asked to create costumes and scenery in your head? In searching for answers to such questions you begin to widen your knowledge of theatre, and to learn the art of criticism and appreciation. In a difficult or obscure play you have to search hard to discover what you are being asked to do.

Theatrical communication is a two-way process. The audience may be fidgety, attentive or spell-bound. Its laughter, shouts and applause affect the performers; its silence is powerful in its expressiveness. As an individual you bring to the theatre all the prejudices, preferences and expectations your experience has taught you. These affect your response to the play and to the rest of the audience. Only you will know if you understood the play, if it said something to you and if you enjoyed yourself or not. The reasons depend on what was brought to the performance by the production team, the actors, the rest of the audience and you. At the end of a performance, something has happened in the world. Whether the same play is performed again in a few hours' time or not, that something is unique.

Rather than analyse the role of the audience in different kinds of productions, I offer here as a case-study an account of a performance I attended. The play was Shakespeare's *Macbeth* which I had seen many times before and studied closely. The production impressed me so much that I was fully aware, at the end, that the performance had significantly added to my experience, changing, minimally but perceptibly, my response to the theatre and the world.

Shakespeare's *Macbeth* at The Warehouse, London, November 1978

The Occasion

Seats for this production were valuable. They did not cost as much as seats in many other London theatres, but there were few of them. I was lucky enough to go by the box-office the very day two extra matinées were scheduled. I arrived on the day, feeling excited and more privileged than usual at entering the theatre.

The Royal Shakespeare Company was mounting the production in repertory. That meant that only a limited number of performances were scheduled, and the actors were busy rehearsing and performing in other plays. The management could not respond to the popularity of the production by simply extending the run. On the other hand, the repertory system had meant that this experimental production could be mounted without total risk. (Only a couple of years later they were to mount their phenomenally successful *Nicholas Nickleby*, which might not have succeeded at all in the commercial theatre, for it played to partly empty houses for many weeks before it caught on and tickets became like gold dust. Later, both these productions were televised, bringing them to much larger audiences, but somewhat diluting the total effect.) The production had had not months, but years, for word of mouth to spread its reputation. It had first been mounted in August 1976 at Stratford-upon-Avon where about half the RSC productions originated.

The Place
Part of the reason there were few tickets was that the production was not mounted at the RSC's main London theatre (which was the Aldwych, holding over 1000 people). Instead it was at the Donmar Warehouse, which was, as you might guess, a building converted to theatrical use. The need for the RSC to have such a theatre was part of a trend in the English theatre of the 1970s towards smaller, more informal theatre spaces than the traditional West End theatres provided. In Shakespeare's own time, the large Globe theatre was for the general population, while the smaller Blackfriars was more select and expensive. This situation had now been reversed. The plushy West End theatres became associated with the posher, lavish aspects of theatre, while small, undecorated, less luxurious theatres suited audiences who did not want the activity of going to the theatre to be associated with snobbery and ostentation. Therefore, the RSC used two alternative spaces, The Other Place, in Stratford-upon-Avon and the Donmar Warehouse in London. (Now its London base is the Barbican Theatre with an experimental space called The Pit.) Many were attracted to the intimacy of these small-scale theatre spaces who might not be so drawn to productions in their larger theatres. For many theatre-goers it is hard to relate to action happening hundreds of feet away, while the actor/audience relationship in a place like the Warehouse was so strong you could be directly aware of it.

The Warehouse held about 150 seats, arranged rather like the inn-yards of Shakespeare's time, with seats on one long side and two short sides, and one gallery. The seats were not reserved (first come, first served) and consisted of wooden benches with cushioning, not individual seats. More like a sports hall, laboratory or lecture room than the cinema type of seats of many theatres.

The Actors

The actors were all experienced professionals most of whom had performed in Shakespeare many times. Since the RSC was one of the most famous and successful theatre companies in the world, they could feel confident of a large amount of prestige, and a respectable salary at least for that theatre season. Working in a company like this can provide a ladder up the profession. At least two members of the cast (Roger Rees as Malcolm, Bob Peck as Macduff) went on to play leading parts in the RSC and other companies. The leading players (Ian McKellen as Macbeth, Judi Dench as Lady Macbeth) had performed many great roles in and out of Shakespeare. Although a stage career does not carry the fame, glory and riches of an idol of screen or pop music, they were both established stars of the theatre, able to attract audiences to themselves as well as to the whole production.

In modern Britain, the training of an actor has not been laid down. This cast included a number of different starting-points: for Ian McKellen an English degree from Cambridge University (which had fostered several leading members of the RSC, including its artistic director Trevor Nunn); for Judi Dench training at the Central School of Speech and Drama, the second oldest acting school in Britain; for Bob Peck, the amateur theatre, for Roger Rees training at art school. (Sometimes the theatre runs through a family – a contemporary of Judi Dench's at acting school was Vanessa Redgrave, whose family now spans four generations of theatre.)

While the repertoire of modern British theatre is very large, and film and television offer other rich opportunities, success in Shakespeare is still the touchstone of achievement for many actors. It is also a measure of its continuity. It is said that after the Commonwealth in England (1642–60) when theatre was banned, one of the first actors to play Hamlet (Thomas Betterton) was coached by someone who had been in Shakespeare's company. Since then the Shakespearean tradition has been unbroken, in that each actor who has played Hamlet (or Macbeth, in this case) has had the opportunity to see others play it first. Ian McKellen may have seen Laurence Olivier or Alec Guinness play it. Similarly Judi Dench might have seen Vivien Leigh or

Simone Signoret play Lady Macbeth. Bob Peck, who played Macduff in this production, has since played Macbeth himself. Thus the tradition is handed on – like a tribal ritual. But it is a tradition that has thrived more on reinterpretation than on slavish imitation of a predecessor.

The Text

Macbeth is a strange and powerful play. First performed in James I's reign it is often thought to have been influenced by that monarch's interest in witchcraft as well as by the fact that he came from Scotland. It is a story of regicide (the killing of a king). In this it links with the deepest anthropological roots of myth. The king represented the whole kingdom. When he was evil, the country's condition was horrific. Shakespeare emphasised the dreadful plight of Scotland under the rule of Macbeth, who killed the rightful king and usurped the throne. He also stressed the importance of safeguarding the future through the continuity of a kingly line. So the shape of the story had links with many mythical structures.

It is also a story of temptation to evil. Macbeth starts off as an honoured and honourable man. He murders the king through ambition, encouraged by three witches, who prophesy that he will be king, and by his wife, who goads him to take the necessary practical steps to fulfil the prophecy. Once started on a life of crime, he goes further and further into it, eventually instigating the murder of a totally innocent woman and her children. This makes the story of great interest psychologically, while also introducing an element of the supernatural.

When Macbeth's evil influence becomes intolerable, Macduff, one of the chief lords of the country, runs off to England in search of Malcolm the rightful heir. Together they return and vanquish Macbeth; Macduff kills him and Malcolm becomes the new King of Scotland. In archaic myths, disasters in the community very often had to be sorted out by divine forces, but here, human forces are just as important in restoring good.

There is a mass of criticism you can read about *Macbeth*, accessible and illuminating to audiences, actors, designers and directors. (The partnership between academic work and theatre production has strengthened during the twentieth century.) There is also strong theatrical tradition unique to this play. *Macbeth* is an unlucky play. People in the theatre know this so well that they very rarely call it by name, preferring, by custom or superstition, to refer to 'the Scottish play'. Theatrical folklore also says that it is very unlucky to quote from the play inside a theatre. One sinister explanation of what is known as 'the *Macbeth* curse', is that the play was a ritual of the black art. The witches are certainly temptations to evil. Their prophecies are equivocal – that is they do not convey a straight truth. For example, they tell Macbeth that 'none of woman born shall harm Macbeth' but their prophecy has a catch. When he tells it to Macduff, Macduff responds triumphantly:

> Despair thy charm,
> And let the angel whom thou still hast served,
> Tell thee, Macduff was from his mother's womb untimely ripped.
>
> (Act v, Scene viii, l. 13)

In other words, Macduff was not born in the strict sense of the word, but had a Caesarean birth.

The play is rich with associations of good and bad forces, including the fact that the English king was said to be healing people through his touch (a custom which King James had revived). It has also been said that it was in itself an enactment of a ritual, with the witches winding up the spell, and spinning three rounds of nine. (There are 27 scenes in *Macbeth*, give or take an extra battle scene.) This interpretation may seem too far-fetched to be believable. However, it is important to remember that even apparently 'civilised' drama may have ritualistic undertones which give it a power for good (or evil) beyond rational explanation.

Costume and Scenic Effect

In this production, as in many modern professional theatres, the costumes and scenery were designed long before the actors started rehearsing, anticipating, to some extent, their approach to interpretation. There are several distinct possibilities open to the designer of a modern Shakespearean production. You could dress it and set it according to the location and period of the story, in this case, eleventh-century Scotland. This is the kind of historical authenticity that was not sought until Victorian times. Shakespeare himself did not cater for such exactitude, so you are actually adding a dimension which might turn out to be a distraction. (I have seen several productions where Macbeth's Viking-like horned helmet and thick beard were distracting, and where Lady Macbeth's headband was authentically low in her brow and looked extremely comical.) Another choice which began to be adopted in the twentieth century was to use the dress of Shakespeare's own period, that is Jacobean. This approach is authentic in another way. Because we think of that period as being highly decorative and elegant, it is used most often for Shakespearean comedy. Here again, the costumes could distract from the show.

A third approach is a return to an earlier convention – to dress the play in the period of the production. In the twentieth century this approach was first adopted in the 1930s. It too is authentic in that it agrees with Shakespeare's own theatrical tradition, when the dress of the time was worn, with minor changes and additions. For some actors and audiences, this approach helps to bridge the gap between Shakespeare's time and ours. However, the incongruity of seeing Shakespeare's characters dressed like the man in the street makes others feel uncomfortable. Weapons, particularly, cause a problem. The idea of killing Macbeth with a pistol instead of sword seems rather absurd.

Modern designers have often been even bolder, selecting a quite different time and place in which to set the play, unjustified by the story, the Shakespearean period or the present, but justified by a useful parallel which might be drawn between the situations and themes of the play. For example *The Merchant of Venice* has been set in the late nineteenth century when Jewish mercantile banking was a distinct social feature; *Julius Caesar* in a modern South American state where democracy and dictatorship compete as forms of government; *Hamlet* set in formal Edwardian society when Hamlet's unseemly behaviour could be shown to be an embarrassment through his inappropriate dress. The Japanese film director Kurosawa made a very effective version of *Macbeth*, called *Throne of Blood*, which placed the situation in the period of the Samurai warriors. There have also been designs which aim for a more abstract approach, but the human body is definitely *not* abstract, so costumes which are too far-fetched are apt to look ridiculous. Some designers now combine several styles and periods within one production.

It is clear that costume design can dominate the concept of a production as much as scenic effect. Yet, as we have seen, Shakespeare's language and theatrical action can create many of the visual effects that are needed. Therefore, some directors and actors have hankered for a way to free Shakespeare from the shackles of the designer. The RSC particularly, had been experimenting with ways to let language and action do the work it was meant to do. With this background in mind, let us now go back to that November afternoon to see what solutions this particular group of people had come up with in reinterpreting *Macbeth* so successfully.

Entering the theatre or converted warehouse, whose walls were painted black, I found the actors already visible on stage. Where the auditorium ended and the stage began was unclear. The empty floor space was the stage, and walking across it to find a seat, I was inevitably sharing it with the actors who were quietly preparing, like the audience, for the play to begin. There was no setting as such, but a black circle painted on the floor, with some upturned wooden crates around it, defined the acting area. The actors were not wearing any elaborate costumes; but neither were they dressed like the members of the audience. All were in black or grey, linking them as a group, and expressing the blackness of the play we were about to experience. What they were wearing were the most suitable clothes in which to rehearse the play. Judi Dench wore a full-length skirt, as many actresses do when they are going to be dressed in period in the final production. Her hair was tied up in a scarf, peasant style, so that no modern style distracted from her concentration or ours. The men wore turtle-neck sweaters and long boots – again the sort of gear an actor might choose, or ask to be given, when rehearsing a period play. Instead of feeling cheated out of lavish visual effects, I felt even more privileged,

Costumes for Lady Macbeth – Sarah Siddons (18th century). Sybil
Thorndike, Komaki Kuihara (20th century)

as if we in the audience had been specially invited to watch a rehearsal behind closed doors.

When the play began, some of the actors not needed in each scene sat on the wooden crates watching, like us. They thus became partially members of the audience, and we the audience seemed to become partially participants, witnesses to the action as it unfolded. This approach was like Brecht's idea of theatre, reminding us that we were all in the real world, but the lack of scene changes was also reminiscent of medieval drama. That circular space represented castle, battlefield and house, indoors and outdoors, Scotland or England. What unified it, was that it symbolised the earth, and earthly time. When Lady Macduff realised she was going to die, she resigned herself to her fate and said:

> But I remember now
> I am in this earthly world, where to do harm
> Is often laudable, to do good sometime
> Accounted dangerous folly.
>
> (Act iv, Scene ii, l. 74)

Never before had I heard those lines so clearly. As she stood in that circle, looking out to the walls of the warehouse that enclosed us all, I knew she included *us* in that comment on the world.

In some ways the production style resembled Chinese theatre. Although the play had supernatural elements which have offered designers the challenge and opportunities to create marvellous effects – witches who vanished, a ghost who appeared only to Macbeth and disappeared – here there were no conjuring tricks. No clouds of dry ice enveloped the actresses and concealed their exits. We had already accepted the convention that the black circle defined the play-world. Therefore, when they were no longer in it, they had vanished. We too were invisible, unless the actors demanded our presence, as in Lady Macduff's lines, which projected beyond the circle, and in the Porter's speech which was addressed to us directly. It was like Chinese theatre too, in that stage management was visible. If an actor needed a prop, he or she fetched it, from the area outside the circle. If a sound effect was needed, the actors created it.

Interpretation

All this was interesting, but what lifted the production on to a level of inspiration, was that the acting, the production and the text were inextricably bound together, creating new meanings that were at the same time old. The poet T. S. Eliot wrote that the experience of great art strikes one as recognition not as novelty. This was what happened to me at this performance. My reaction was not 'How original!' but 'How right!'

When King Duncan, accepting Macbeth's hospitality, retired for the night, he was disrobed of his regal attire. Appropriately, this was the only real costume in the production, for to be anointed king was to be given a special ceremonial role that brought special powers and responsibilities. (Perhaps if he had not removed it, he would not have been murdered?) At any rate, the royal robes were removed and placed on a dummy at the side of the stage. This symbolised that Scotland was without a king. When Macbeth was crowned, the robes were taken off the dummy and placed on him. But, was he not something of a dummy himself, a kind of puppet king? The play was permeated with imagery about clothes.

When Macbeth was addressed as 'thane of Cawdor' he replied:

> The thane of Cawdor lives: why do you dress me
> In borrow'd robes?
>
> (Act II, Scene iii, l. 108)

After the murder of Duncan, when Ross said he was going to Scone for Macbeth's coronation, Macduff answered:

> Well, may you see things well done there: Adieu!
> Lest our old robes sit easier than our new.
>
> (Act II, Scene iv, l. 37)

Amongst other images of clothes, the most vivid was spoken by Angus, another lord, speaking of Macbeth when he was king:

> now does he feel his title
> Hang loose upon him, like a giant's robe
> Upon a dwarfish thief.
>
> (Act V, Scene ii, l. 20)

Macbeth wore the ceremonial robes until he removed them to fight the forces of Macduff and Malcolm, putting the fate of Scotland in the balance. Draped once again on the dummy, the clothes reminded me that the kingdom had no one to ensure its well-being and prosperity. Finally, after the battle, Malcolm became king and wore the robes.

On the night of the murder of Duncan, there were fearful storms. As in similar circumstances in Shakespeare's *Julius Caesar* and *King Lear*, unruliness on earth was matched by cosmic forces. Instead of using recorded storm effects, here a thunder sheet was used – a huge sheet of metal which rumbled realistically when shaken (the traditional theatrical method of creating a storm before recording was possible). In keeping with the convention of the production, the thunder sheet was visible to the audience and an actor shook it. The actor in question was Ian McKellen, not required in the acting area during that scene. I saw Macbeth himself create the storm. This sight and sound powerfully symbolised that the evils besetting Scotland were through his deeds.

These images were a realisation of Shakespeare's idea that the world is like a theatre, and theatre is like the world. But his characters were not like puppets. In every production of *Macbeth* the same words are spoken, but the motivation they are given, the purpose behind them, modifies the meaning, even changes, however slightly, the story the actors are telling. The quality that allows new discoveries to be made in the meaning is what makes people feel that Shakespeare is always our contemporary.

In the early parts of the play Lady Macbeth had the upper hand in the relationship. This was characterised by Ian McKellen and Judi Dench as a strong sexual power. He seemed to desire her passionately and strove to be worthy of her sexual favours. (Sometimes Lady Macbeth has been played as if she was not sexually passionate herself, because she asked the spirits to unsex her. It was much more convincing when this actress showed that the character had sexual desires which she was willing to sublimate, in order to reach the goal of having her husband be king.) This mutual passion goaded them on, Lady Macbeth taunted him for not being a man, when she thought he was weakening in his intention; she was testing his potency as well as his courage.

But later, Macbeth separated himself from her company, to pursue his black deeds alone. She then experienced a rapid deterioration, took to walking in her sleep, reliving the night of the murder, until she died. Unfortunately for the actress, interesting though her decline was, it was not the main focus of the action, which was rather Macbeth's deterioration and despair. Here, though, I saw more clearly than ever before, the stages of her unhappiness and breakdown.

The reading of one line marked the beginning unequivocally. After his coronation Macbeth dismissed his court, saying:

> Fare well, let every man be master of his time
> Till seven at night; to make society
> The sweeter welcome, we will keep ourself
> Till supper-time alone: while then, God be with you.
>
> (Act iii, Scene i, l. 40)

As he spoke these words all the lords left the acting area. Ian McKellen paused after the word 'alone'. Only Lady Macbeth was left, expecting to enjoy the first moments of mutual congratulation, perhaps celebrating in bed together. He looked at her and spoke the other half of the line, 'while then, God be with you!' indicating that she had misunderstood his words: 'we will keep ourself/Till supper-time alone': He did not mean the two of them, but was using the royal we allowed to his kingly state. The rejection was complete and totally unexpected. Judi Dench flinched, but retired obediently. Throughout the next few scenes, when she was not needed, she sat on her wooden crate looking as if in a state of shock. From this state, she never recovered. In the banquet scene in which Macbeth nearly gave his guilt away, I saw Lady Macbeth trying to cope with this while still upset. Then again, she sat quietly on her crate, waiting for the sleepwalking scene. I saw Judi Dench, preparing, off stage but visibly, to play an important scene. At the same time I saw Lady Macbeth completely isolated and useless, having nothing to do but brood on the terrible deeds they had done.

Despite the number of productions there have been of *Macbeth* a few interesting puzzles remain. For example, Macbeth sent two men to kill his former friend Banquo, but at the scene of the murder they were joined by another who was never identified. There is also a staging problem. Banquo's ghost appeared to Macbeth at the feast held that evening at the castle. He saw the ghost sitting at a place which to everyone else was empty. The ghost vanished, then reappeared again, and the feast broke up in disarray over Macbeth's odd behaviour. These problems were solved by one character, Seyton, a servant not named in the script until near the end. However, in this small-scale production he was more noticeable than usual, being the *only* servant. *He* was the third murderer. *He* sat in the empty seat, momentarily, so that when he was there, all seemed well to Macbeth; when he was not, Macbeth filled the empty space with the illusion of Banquo. Always at hand to 'help' Macbeth he seemed like an evil force himself. His name was remarkably similar to 'Satan'.

Another puzzle was Malcolm's character. He was the rightful heir to Duncan's throne. When he became king, order was restored in Scotland. However, he ran away after his father's murder. Macduff went to England to ask him to come back, to fight Macbeth and to be king. Instead of agreeing, or discussing the problem, he gave Macduff a horrific character sketch of himself, claiming to be sexually avaricious and far more cruel and tyrannical than Macbeth. Just when Macduff was in total despair, Malcolm recanted this 'confession' and said he was just testing Macduff. He agreed to what Macduff had been asking, they returned to Scotland, and all seemed well. But what I saw was Macduff's reaction to Malcolm's account of himself. In Bob Peck's face I saw all trust destroyed, never to be restored. He seemed to be thinking 'Either this man lied the first time, or he lied the second time. I don't know which, but I'll never be able to put my confidence in him as a just ruler.' When the moment came to place the royal robes on Malcolm, there was no guarantee that evil had been defeated. This was the sombrest ending I had ever seen for this play. When evil is let loose in the world, can it be redeemed? 'What's done is done'. By attending another performance of *Macbeth* I had witnessed 'a deed without a name'.

10

The functions of theatre

WHEN we have studied the art of theatre from several different aspects, we are then in a position to look and see how the separate parts are blended to make the whole. This chapter both draws the parts together and examines the drawing-together, leading towards the questions: What place does theatre hold in social life? and how does it function?

There are three kinds of ingredients in a theatrical performance. First there are the basic conditions which must exist for it to happen: Time, Place, Actors, The Play. Secondly, there are the elements that go to make up the art of theatre: Mask and Costume, Movement and Speech, Scenery and Lighting, Music and Sound. Thirdly, there is the Reception of the performance by those present, through watching and listening. Each of these ingredients involves one or more functions. These functions may require a number of people to carry them out, but this is not always the case, as previous chapters have shown. Let us examine further how the tasks are shared out. Some of the ground to be covered should now be familiar. Having gone over it, you may find other ways of describing and defining the collective art of theatre.

The occasion

If the occasion is a religious festival, appropriate members of the community may have regular preparations to make; for example, priests or elders may have to select the date according to their special knowledge. Similarly, if the occasion is a secular celebration, the community knows how to set about preparing for it. Often, over the years, secular, seasonal, and religious celebrations merge together; for example, at Carnival time before Lent begins in parts of Europe and America.

There are many occasions in modern society – as there were in primitive communities, and still are in the surviving ones – when theatre is used in specific fields of work, in education, training and therapy. Here, too, the appropriate members of the community, such as teachers and healers, must make the necessary arrangements. When theatre is used for general entertainment, not arranged for a special occasion, the selection and announcing of the time may require planning and a good deal of publicity. On the other hand, the occasion may be spontaneous, with very little preparation. Perhaps an actor simply enters, creates a space and begins, just as a child simply begins to play.

Arranging the occasion often involves finding the money for it. In the entertainment industry, the people who find the money are the producers. In Britain, they may be called managers. With commercial profit as their motive, they may employ a formidable array of staff, both inside and outside the theatre, to organise the budgeting, recruit the artists and staff, find financial backers, market the product and handle the revenue.

Within the modern professional theatre, there exists the possibility of a permanent company, which is organised to mount whole seasons of productions. And these are often financed by a combination of funding: from government sources, such as the Arts Council of Great Britain; from sponsoring organisations, such as banks, which want to enhance their public image; and from ticket sales. The producer's function, then, is split into many parts. A veritable bureaucracy of theatre can grow up around a theatre.

Whether there is a producer, or a team of producers, a group of priests or a medicine man, a Master of the Revels, or an educational or health establishment, the function of producing, managing and organising the event must happen. Even an actor who performs spontaneously may well need to pass the hat round afterwards, fulfilling the function of being his/her own box office staff.

Space

One of the amateur actors in *A Midsummer Night's Dream* looked at what was supposed to be a clearing in the Athenian forest and said 'Here's a marvellous convenient place for our rehearsal' (Act III, Scene i, l. 2). He saw at a glance that the patch of ground offered the needs of a stage. He had found a 'theatre' and was in a sense its designer. Whether a theatre is purpose-built, either as a temporary structure or a permanent playhouse, or whether it is converted to theatrical use, one or more people have designed and constructed it. Often, this has meant following some long-established tradition about where the theatre space is or what it is like. At other times, the design and construction have been huge feats of architecture, often experimental, as with the Theatre in London built in 1576, or the Total Theatre of the Bauhaus, an avant-garde invention of 1927 which was never actually built. Theatre architecture has not by any means moved progressively towards greater sophistication. A desire for simplicity has run alongside a desire for grander buildings. There have always been, and will continue to be, open-air theatres and temporary structures set up in village squares; barns and warehouses, classrooms, halls and other useful spaces converted into theatres; an attic or basement that offers the possibility of a tiny theatre. But large or small, indoor or outdoor, temporary or permanent, someone, at some point, has to set aside the place where the play will be done.

Participants and observers

In China, a member of the Pear Orchard was a highly trained professional. In tribal communities, everyone at some point will participate in the enactment of a dramatised ritual. An actor may be a famous 'star' commanding a huge fortune whenever he or she appears on the stage. Another may be a struggling professional who has spent most of his career 'resting' (or out-of-work); another a busy amateur; another a schizophrenic patient, persuaded for a few minutes to act out, for therapeutic reasons, a painful relationship with another person. These are all actors, either by profession, inclination, or temporary agreement.

For theatre to occur, two kinds of involvement are necessary – participation and observation. This would seem to suggest that one or more people must be actors, and one or more people must be spectators or audience. This distinction is seen by some theorists as a basic difference between 'theatre', and other kinds of enactment, such as ritual, children's play or educational drama. However, I do not think the distinction is clear enough to be useful to us. At any particular moment in a play, one character may be the focus of attention, while others are watching and reacting, just like the audience. The same is true of tribal ritual. Sometimes within a play the audience are given a role. In Peter Shaffer's *Amadeus* for example, they are the ghosts of the future, in Christmas pantomime they are often cast as the friend of a comic or virtuous character, and must shout out or warn when something untoward is about to happen. In an improvisational drama lesson, the teacher may cast the whole class as 'villagers'. Those who take a passive role in the improvisation, observing what goes on but taking little part, can still be classed as participants in the drama. Thus in many instances the same people may interchange between being actors and audience. However, it must be understood and agreed (by convention or mutual acceptance) that whoever is acting a role in the play is licensed to step out of their everyday sphere to perform in it. Even in situations where the actor plays him/herself, as a patient in psychodrama, or a trainee or student practising an interview situation, the licence to perform must have been granted formally or informally, allowing them to explore possible modes of their own behaviour without restraint.

The number of actors may be one, or many. So may the number of audience. In some religious drama the only 'audience' may be the god(s). In Thailand, for example, the family of a recently deceased person traditionally offer a play which is performed without an audience. Could one person be both actor and audience? In other words can 'theatre' happen with only one person present? The question may seem absurd, but the answer is really a philosophical one. If 'person' can split into parts – Ego and Id, Good Conscience and Bad Conscience, Child-self and Parent-self – then it is possible to conceive of a solo performance in which someone acts out a situation which he/she simultaneously observes.

Script – play – dramatised story

Actors' skills may often be put to other uses than to present a play. Many languages do not distinguish clearly in their vocabulary between a player, a story-teller, juggler, minstrel, acrobat, singer, clown or other kind of entertainer, unless the art has developed a high degree of specialisation. The chief characteristic of a play is that a story is told through actors dramatising it.

A common word for an actor is Thespian, after the Ancient Greek who, according to records, first took on a dramatic role in order to tell the story. The French word for an actor is *comédien*, which confuses things to some extent because he/she may be a tragedian, but the word is attached to anyone playing out a dramatised situation.

A playwright is needed then, to create the dramatised story. As we have seen, stories arise from out of the community, and mimicry from those who are skilled at it. Even if a playwright strives for originality, the ideas and the behaviour imitated will still be a reflection of the community in which he/she lives. The word playwright does not necessarily mean someone who *writes* plays. He or she is a craftsman who makes a story into a playable form. It is not always necessary to have this function performed by a separate person. In many forms of drama, the performers create the play. In ritualised drama, the form of the play is often buried so far in the past that no one knows who created it, perhaps a priest, shaman or medicine-man, or a series of them who gradually refined it. Or perhaps the ordinary members of the community. It is handed down through hearsay or experience, often without people quite knowing the rhyme or reason for it. For example, Mummers' plays in England contain a mixture of mumbo-jumbo and anachronistic addition (such as having Napoleon in a play about St George). In improvised plays, too, no single playwright is needed. In the *commedia dell'arte* tradition, various scenarios, or skeleton scenes, were used as a basis for the performance, rather as a group of inventive cooks might search through the larder and combine known ingredients to create a new dish, adding an original spice perhaps, to bring a unique flavour to it. In other forms of improvised drama, especially in educational or experimental work, the actors control the play as it goes along, perhaps with a leader to steer the course.

But a vast number of plays have been written and/or consciously devised for performance by one person, or by two or more working together. Even in forms of drama which are in some ways traditional, like the medieval mystery plays, or the drama, the scripts that have come down to us are written by individual playwrights. The Wakefield Master who wrote one Corpus Christi cycle is not known by name but his characteristic style and shaping influence is noticeable. The greatest *Noh* writer, Zeami, contributed greatly to the flowering of this form of drama, just as Shakespeare and his contemporary writers helped to bring Renaissance drama in England to its great peak at the turn of the 1600s.

Ironically, the periods of great written drama have not always coincided with periods of great performance and productions. In Europe, the eighteenth-century professional theatre produced outstanding actors, and scenic developments progressed, but the written drama was less impressive, until the second half of the nineteenth century when it burgeoned with writers such as Ibsen, Strindberg, Chekhov and Shaw.

Although surviving written drama is only a fragment of the plays that have been and are being performed around the world, and although it cannot give us the full flavour of performance, it is nevertheless an impressive record of the ways in which life and beliefs have been shaped into theatrical form in different times and places throughout the world. Until about a hundred years ago the import and export of drama was rare. Also, except for a few particularly admired plays or playwrights, such as Shakespeare, or the *Noh* repertoire, established theatre companies tended to perform only plays of their own period. Nowadays, with the huge printed output of plays from different periods and places, we have the choice of world drama available to us, to explore, reperform or adapt where and when we see fit.

Scenic effect

We have looked at scenery and props created out of nothing by the actor, or simple screens and selected objects transformed by the power of imagination evoked by the actors. In these cases much of the work of scenic artists is done by actors and audience. Nevertheless, even the simplest performance usually requires some arrangement of the stage, some supervision of the technical details, to ensure that all goes smoothly. The person who performs this is the stage-manager. Except in the most informal circumstances, such as in a class or session where the leader can stop the proceedings without there being any loss of dignity, such a person is needed. They may or may not be performing some other function as well. In Chinese theatre the stage-manager or property master appeared on the stage as part of the dramatic action. Since the scenery was simple his tasks were mainly related to looking after the properties, placing them correctly on stage or handing them to actors. When this form of theatre first became known in the West, the public appearance of the stage-manager was a novelty, because it broke the illusion of a consistent, self-contained fictional world on the stage. However, the idea has now been imitated in European and American plays. In Thornton Wilder's play, *Our Town* (1938), one of the characters is the stage-manager. (Ironically though, the actor does not usually combine this role with the tasks of a 'real' stage-manager!)

In Chinese and Japanese theatre, any scene changing that was necessary was done by stage-hands visible to the audience. This convention too, has now been introduced into some productions in the West. Sometimes costumed actors will now change the scenes; often this is done in a semi-realistic convention: for example, actors playing servants may change the scene 'as if' performing tasks within their role. But it is no longer an offence to theatrical convention in the West, for the audience to see the stage-hands and watch the set being changed during scene-breaks. In each production there is a choice whether to lower the curtain, or have a black-out, or let the change be visible.

From all that has been said of scenic effects in European theatre history, it is clear that the mechanics and technology have involved countless numbers of people from set-builders to lighting designers, sound crew, stage crews, property masters and stage-management teams. Costume makers and wardrobe staff are also part of the production team. The simplest way of allotting tasks has been to have one group of people building the show, under the supervision of a designer – if there is one – and another group running it, under the supervision of the stage-manager. One group prepares the production; their work finishes at the moment when the performance begins. The other group takes over to service it from immediately before to immediately after the performance.

The operation of a technically complicated production is considerable. It is no wonder that there has sometimes been tension in the theatre between 'techies' and 'talent' – the actors. This is the workaday manifestation of the conflict mentioned in Chapter 7, where some feel that the scenery, lighting, costumes and special effects are the most important part of theatrical effect, while others want the theatre to be 'two boards and a passion'. Nowadays the term 'poor theatre' is sometimes used to describe deliberately simple presentation that relies on the actors. The word is used ironically, not to be disparaging or to comment on lack of finance. On the other hand, some audiences who go to the great metropolises of the world want to be entertained with a real show. When deciding what play to see, you are often choosing between several styles of presentation, as well as between plays and actors on offer.

Music and sound effects

Sound effects are part of the technical side of theatre. Whether live or recorded, the effects are operated under the general supervision of the stage-manager, who may require several assistant stage-managers (ASMs) to carry out all the backstage tasks.

With music, the variety of functions is considerable. Although music is not an essential part of theatre, it is surprising how few performances actually contain none at all, though it may be simply a few bars of recorded music played before the play begins, or during the interval. The largest number of different roles associated with music is probably in the American musicals. Here, the composer, the lyricist, the choreographer and the scriptwriter may all be separate people. You then add the orchestrator, and the musical director who may or may not conduct the show, before even reaching the musicians and the rehearsal pianist. When it comes to amplification, sound technicians are involved. Clearly the biggest factors are whether the music is specially composed for the production, whether it is live or recorded. If a musical production is revived, whether opera, ballet or musical, the original score is as important as the script of a classical play. Sometimes when music is not so integral to the piece, new music is composed even when a score already exists. Grieg's incidental music to Ibsen's *Peer Gynt* is rarely used in performance, any more than the original set design. But no one would think of doing *The Magic Flute*, *Swan Lake* or *West Side Story* without using the scores of Mozart, Tchaikovsky and Leonard Bernstein, and also as much as possible of Petipa's or Jerome Robbins's choreography.

The invisible function of theatre

Unlike the painter, the actor cannot see what he is creating, except in front of a mirror, or hear the effect as well as a musician playing an instrument. Even at the simplest level, when only one or two actors are involved, an outside eye and ear is often needed when a performance is to take place. This invisible function may be to train the performer, either in specific skills or for a specific performance. From participants of tribal rituals, to the opera singer performing in another language, teachers and trainers have been needed in theatre, sometimes established in theatre academies, sometimes simply a parent or elder instructing a child to take over a role in the community drama.

Where a production has some complexity, someone is needed to oversee the rehearsals and perhaps the performance itself. One painting of a medieval drama depicted a kind of master of ceremonies conducting the proceedings like a musical conductor with a script and baton. More often this function is filled invisibly or half-invisibly. In some opera houses, a prompt box is placed in the centre down-stage, below the stage-floor level, and you may sometimes glimpse the prompt mouthing the words to keep the singer/actors on the word and beat. That all-embracing role of the stage-manager includes the preparation of the prompt-book, the bible of theatrical performances. In many theatres the stage-manager's supervisory position has meant that he or she ran the rehearsals, though there might also be some other overseer, such as a Master of the Revels, the playwright, or a leading actor who took precedence and gave commands.

In the late nineteenth and early twentieth centuries, however, there emerged in the European theatre a new role for the fulfilment of this invisible function. That was the producer (English term) or director (American term). (To avoid confusion, the American terminology is now more common, the producer being the organiser of the event, and the director the person who guides the direction of the performance on stage.) Partly the need arose because of the greater complexity of production, especially when lighting design was introduced. Partly the needs of realism demanded it; for if the whole effect on stage was to be authentic and consistent, co-ordination of all aspects of the production became much more important. Lastly, the gradual increase in knowledge and experience of other forms of theatre gave far more freedom of interpretation, style and convention. Someone had to exercise choice and although an experienced actor can and still does, achieve the ability both to act and to perceive the whole, he/she will often choose not to fulfil both functions.

The sort of questions that have to be decided if Shakespeare's *Hamlet* is to be put on include: should it be done in Elizabethan style, or with the full paraphernalia of illusionistic production evoking medieval Denmark, or with modernistic designs influenced by abstract art? And should the prince be interpreted as a romantic, passionate, melancholy lover, or as a witty intellectual, or a psychological problem? All these possibilities have arisen in the twentieth century over the interpretation of one play. No one convention or interpretation served the whole community any more and yet a unanimity of vision was considered desirable.

The director's concept now tends to dominate many productions, especially of classic plays which are being reinterpreted. His or her function often overlaps with the designer's, the playwright's, the stage-manager's, the acting coach's and perhaps the leading actor's. Basically he or she functions as that outside eye or ear, 'an audience of one', as the great director Tyrone Guthrie put it. In simpler communities than those of the modern industrialised world, the invisible function was filled by past traditions, a unified system of beliefs and culture, even by religious knowledge. Even now, a cohesive group can mount a production without direction, but the task will involve a conscious search for that cohesion, for methods of working as an ensemble, for creating a collective piece of theatre.

The role of the theatre director has emerged in Europe during the last hundred years. Directors were often experimental, seeking new ways to fulfil a vision of what they thought the art of theatre could be. Several have spread their new ideas throughout the world. Examples of influential directors include: from Russia, Eugene Vakhtangov (1883–1922), Alexander Tairov (1885–1950) and Nikolai Okhlopkov (1900–67); from France, André Antoine (1858–1943) and Jacques Copeau (1879–1949); from Germany, Max Reinhardt (1873–1943); from England, Harley Granville-Barker (1877–1946), Tyrone Guthrie (1900–71) and Peter Brook (1925–); the Swedish director Ingmar Bergman (1918–); and the Polish director Jerzy Grotowski (1933–). These, and many other eminent directors all over the world, not only put their own stamp on many productions, but helped to establish a new role in the theatre.

Within the history of theatre, many individuals have achieved fame, making a contribution to the art of theatre, expanding its possibilities. You can study the work of actors, playwrights, architects and designers, directors and producers. Yet, in the final analysis it is the collective nature of theatre that characterises it most, creating a total experience out of a ragbag of different arts and skills, like the motley coat of the traditional fool.

As we draw to the end of this introduction to theatre, let us gather the strands together and assess the different characteristics, contrasts and similarities world theatre has shown in cultures far separated in time and place. There are several different ways we might assess a theatre event.

Accessibility

When considering any piece of theatre, it will be useful to examine what kind of audience it is reaching out to. Often people will draw a distinction between popular theatre and theatre which eliminates all but a few from its audience, the elite. Yet, seen in world terms, this distinction becomes blurred.

Fertility rites of different tribes involved the whole community, but they were at the same time esoteric and obscure. An example of popular but inaccessible theatre is the traditional British Christmas pantomime. This has such mass appeal that it is the *one* form of theatre many people go to – as part of the secular/religious seasonal festival of Christmas. But it is surprisingly difficult to explain its characteristics to others: a play based on a nursery tale in which men and women reverse roles, and which includes an audience song and other forms of participation, with music and spectacular scenery and topical jokes that may be quite risky – either because they are blue, or because they are political. This mish-mash of traditional entertainment has evolved over many generations but it is often incomprehensible, even to other English-speaking peoples.

Traditional plays are part of a popular culture. They assume knowledge and experience both of form and of content. They are therefore inaccessible without explanation to people from another culture. Other factors may limit the number of people who can enjoy a play. Although a play in another language is difficult to understand, this does not stop many people from enjoying opera performed in a foreign language. Grand opera is considered elitist entertainment in many cultures, yet in Italy, the homeland of Guiseppe Verdi, working people attend with real enjoyment. But other kinds of language may also be too specialised – the language of behaviour for example. A comedy of manners, a play which ridicules social behaviour, may be obscure and unfunny to those who do not know such manners. (In England, Restoration comedy and the plays of Oscar Wilde and Nöel

Coward are famous examples of comedy of manners, but equally, a comedy about rastafarians in Brixton might not be accessible to other groups.) Fringe theatre, because it is cheap, is often said to reduce elitism, but the venues are small, and the type of play often attracts a minority audience. A play may be too intellectual for one type of audience, too vulgar for another. Its social message may be unacceptable to some, while a topical play may quickly lose significance even in its own community.

The fact is that every form of theatre cuts out as many as it attracts. Each has a cult following: those who either through tradition, personal experience or study can get in tune with what the actors are communicating. This makes the audience's role in the theatre crucial. If there are insufficient people at a performance who are in touch with what the play is about, then the whole event begins to lose momentum. If you listen to a comedian whose jokes are falling flat, you will often find that his performance begins to sound strained and full of effort.

It should not surprise us that every play is more accessible to some groups than to others, even when it has evolved as a popular expression. It is more surprising how many plays can overcome the divisions of culture, intellect and education. Shakespeare continues to be an inspiration for revivals and adaptations; drama written two thousand years ago in Athens still has power to move audiences; archaic rituals fascinate outsiders privileged to see them; Ibsen is performed in Japan; and every tourist to China hopes to see the Peking Opera. All these examples show us that theatre can provide a channel of communication that will unite people across years and space more than reason can explain.

So patterns of accessibility are complicated; they depend on previous knowledge and experience, and also on openness to what the actor is communicating. The performance of a play may not only confirm our beliefs, but expand them. In any performance be open to what seems to be being demanded of you, and be willing to give it.

Illusions of reality

Much of this book has examined the different approaches to

realism – the imitation of reality – that have been adopted in different conventions of theatre. In particular the contrast between Eastern, Western and Third World traditions, which in the twentieth century have become available to both cultures. To delve into this matter very deeply would bring us quickly into the field of philosophy. But since all discussions of theatre come down to illusion and reality, it is necessary at least to embark upon some aspects of this duality.

In the West a tradition developed whereby you could to a great extent pretend that what you were watching was real life. Theatre imitated surface reality – through its scenic effects – its plausible dialogue and characters, and its performers striving to behave 'as if' the situation was really happening. This convention split off the stage from the auditorium. In the Eastern tradition, what you experienced was more like a theatrical ceremony. The trappings of the theatre were much more visible than any attempt to show a replica of the fictional place and characters. This is the contrast between two ways of imitating reality. Other traditions such as African folk drama, Greek and medieval, showed variations on these styles. However, in this 'world view', I wish to show what even these widely contrasted methods have in common.

In the Western tradition, the darkening of the auditorium helped to remove distractions, so that the audience could become quite absorbed in the dramatic experience. When Brecht criticised this style he objected to the way the audience were swept out of themselves, and welcomed the Eastern style which kept the audience conscious of their real selves. However, his interpretation may not have been the correct one. Let us look at it another way, with some awareness of the Eastern approach to reality. For an audience influenced by Buddhism, the world of everyday things was an illusion. To them, the trappings of surface realism were just as much a distraction as the trappings of visible stage-management were to the conventional Western audience.

What we find in common between the two traditions is this desire not to distract the audience from the essence of what is going on. The truth of a play is not about scenery. Building a set that looks like a real room may help to show the audience some truths about space, possessions, social and psychological conditions. But what if you start to wonder if the walls are solid, if the actor really stammers or is doing it for the part, or how they make the stage telephone ring at the appropriate moment? The illusionistic theatre of the West is like a wonderful conjuring trick, which *may* convince, if presented skilfully enough, but may simply arouse curiosity about how it was done, creating a distraction, and especially for an audience for whom physical reality is not the most important kind. The Eastern theatre did not run that risk. The fan is a fan, the chair is a chair. I have nothing up my sleeve.

The kind of theatre Brecht liked was more like the Christian medieval tradition. In both these styles, the aim was to focus the audience on the important truth – that this matters to *you*, personally (whether that truth was religious or social). For that reason, both traditions kept on reminding the audience of their real presence.

So we distinguish three levels of reality in theatre:

(1) the reality of here and now where the audience and actors are united;
(2) the illusionary reality, the fiction that is built up by the arts of theatre;
(3) the reality beyond, the truth that the play or the whole event is about.

It is a matter of philosophy which level of reality is considered the most illusory of the three, but it is a matter of theatre which level is conveyed to the audience and how.

The magic of theatre

A television series was made about world theatre. The first episode was devoted to the magic of theatre. It showed dancers in Bali, who became so intensively engrossed in what they were doing that they performed magic – cutting each other with swords without drawing blood. And it showed the atmosphere of excitement and glamour at an opening night on Broadway in New York. These are examples of theatre taking us out of our ordinary lives, temporarily creating a special dimension of existence. This aspect of theatre relates somewhat to the previous section, where we talked about the third level of reality beyond the immediate and the fiction. It explains why theatre and dreams have often been paralleled. Shakespeare very often refers in his plays to human life being like a dream:

> We are such stuff
> As dreams are made on; and our little life
> Is rounded with a sleep.
> (*The Tempest*, Act IV, Scene i, l. 156)

and also to theatre:

> Life's but a walking shadow, a poor player
> That struts and frets his hour upon the stage
> And then is heard no more.
> (*Macbeth*, Act v, Scene v, l. 24)

When you enter a theatre, you may feel you are in a different world, where earth-time is suspended for the duration of the play, until at the end you return to normal existence, just as, when you wake from a dream you take up your life again; you remember something of what you experienced in the dream, and even what you do not remember may affect you unconsciously. Archaic people believe in the significance of dreams. The modern rediscovery that the dream-mind tells a kind of truth, entered European awareness after Freud wrote *The Interpretation of Dreams* in 1900. He gave dreams and irrational modes of thought a higher status than they had had before. Antonin Artaud, the Frenchman who had been impressed by Balinese theatre coined the phrase 'theatre of cruelty' to describe how theatre can and should break through the trappings of ordinary logical experience to confront people with a psychedelic (mind-blowing) experience. He had been impressed by the Balinese dancers' power to express something beyond the common sense world.

Experience outside the control of common sense is also madness. A dream, a play, or an ecstasy may give us a vision of some new reality – or it may, like a drug or a madness, bring hallucination and delusion. It may be thought dangerous to break through the normal inhibitions that control our everyday experience. In archaic societies, only under very special conditions is the ecstatic experience allowed, controlled by a *shaman*, witch-doctor, priest or other trained person. In many cultures there have been and still are certain special rites open only to a few selected initiates. In the modern world, psychodrama, and some theatre based on Artaud's 'theatre of cruelty', need to be equally carefully controlled if they are not to prove a danger to the participants and observers. Groups or individuals have to decide for themselves whether the experience of being lost in a make-believe world is an escape from the truth. That is what Puritans believe, and they therefore condemn the theatre. Others believe it, but without disapproving. They accept that theatre is a relief from the harsh truths of living – an interlude in the normal running of events. They believe it may be a well-deserved break, like a holiday.

The glamour of theatre remains an important part of its appeal. Stars of stage and screen are considered special people, who are admired and studied for no other reason than that they are stars (though they often have specific skills and talent as well). The word glamour itself is associated with mystery, magic and fairy land. Although we do not usually think that stars have magical powers, we still use words like 'charm' and cast a 'spell' to describe their effect. (Just as we do not believe, as people have done in the past, that royalty can heal the sick through touch, yet still people throng to get as near as they can, and like to try and touch them.)

Theatre as a view of society

While many seek the magical quality of theatre, others emphasise the continuity between the everyday world and the theatre. After all, many plays deal with exactly the same kind of events, people, problems and solutions that we meet in ordinary life. Theatre is simply an extension of life. Those who prefer this view of theatre regard it as a kind of laboratory. In the theatre, we have the opportunity to examine aspects of reality, including ideas, emotions, wishes, challenges and other abstractions of life, and thereby add to our experience and knowledge. For this approach, the magical aspects of theatre distract us from its truth. This is what Brecht felt, with his belief that we are not to be taken out of ourselves in the theatre, but must keep our wits about us throughout, so as to evaluate the human events and modify our own behaviour accordingly. This attitude to theatre leads to just as much of a split between approval and disapproval. Theatre may be educational in the broadest sense, offering warnings and recommendations for how to conduct our lives. Only if we agree with the lesson will we approve of the play. Plays are often evaluated according to the lesson they teach. This evaluation may apply not only to individual plays, but to a whole group or society. For example, in the early days of the Bolshevik Revolution in Russia, plays that turned normality upside down, or preached revolution, were much approved. But later, when the regime was established, such plays were frowned upon and censored. It became government policy only to approve plays that endorsed what the Socialists had achieved.

So when we come to examine attitudes to the theatre, we find a range of possible responses to two basic notions about theatre. As you examine your own, and other people's attitude to the theatre, and to specific plays, it will be interesting to see how it is placed among the following possible debating positions:

THEATRE IS A WORLD OF DREAMS

Yes –	Yes –	No –
a world of make-believe	a part of reality beyond the everyday world	the same kind of world we all live in

THEATRE IS A GOOD THING

Yes –	No –	Yes –	No –	Yes –	No –
a pleasant escape	a time-wasting occupation	puts us in touch with essential truths	dabbles with things we should leave alone	can teach us how to live our lives	teaches us the wrong things

Variables in theatre

When you see a film such as *Gone With The Wind* or *Star Wars* for the umpteenth time, the performances do not change although the time is different and the place and company may also have changed. In theatre, the time and perhaps the place are different for the performers as well as for the audience. Yet the script, the scenery, the music and the moves may be the same. When it comes to doing a different play, or a different production, there are many more variables.

Theatre, then, is both a unique and a repeatable event. Many people like live theatre because of the very fact that it is spontaneous and changeable. They even relish moments when things go wrong, because such mishaps demonstrate the lifelike uncertainty and uniqueness of the event. Yet its sameness and repeatability are also attractive. In the commercial theatre, you want a guarantee you are getting your money's worth as much as the people who went the night, month or even the year, before. In other kinds of theatre too, repetition is important to maintain effectiveness. One of the important aspects of ritual is repetition: a community does not change its dramas unless there is a reason. As human civilisation has progressed more rapidly, the appetite for change and originality has increased. In producing the mystery plays, the Roman Catholic Church wished to remind its audience of unchanging truths; by Shakespeare's time, those truths no longer seemed permanent, so drama became much more various, and novelty was an attraction.

Because the script is the chief method of recording a theatre event, we tend to think of improvised drama as the most changeable form. But often in companies that specialise in improvisations, the actors, the props, the theatre, and in many traditions, the characters too, remain the same. And when an old play is remounted, it may be very different from the original production. In contrast, two different plays performed by the same company of actors may create quite similar impressions, especially if the scenery and costumes are taken from stock, which may happen either by tradition, as in Japanese theatre, or by economics, as in low-budget repertory companies. In the Comédie Française, the French national theatre, it was for many years a matter of pride that productions of the classics were handed down, virtually unchanged, from generation to generation. In England, the 'infinite variety' of Shakespeare's plays has led to a tradition where any revival is an occasion to look at the script afresh.

Consider your own attitude to the balance of uniqueness and repeatability in the theatre. For my part, I like to think of every performance as an open rehearsal – the French term for a rehearsal is *la répétition*. Each rehearsal is an opportunity both to refine and to reinterpret what has already been done. You can regard life like that too, in its theatre-like quality. Life is not a rehearsal, it is the real thing. But like the theatre, it gives individuals and communities the chance to try a new approach from time to time, or to keep practising the old approach; to redefine roles or to adopt new ones; to reflect on the past and prepare for the future.

> All the world's a stage,
> And all the men and women, merely players;
> They have their exits and their entrances,
> And one man in his time plays many parts,
> His acts being seven ages.
>
> (*As You Like It*, Act II, Scene vii, l. 138)

Research topics and projects

WHENEVER people act out a story or situation intentionally and continuously in a space, you can say that 'theatre' is happening. This means that the art of theatre is a very broad subject. It spans several different disciplines, including anthropology, psychology, history, geography, design and technology, religion and art. The history of theatre is a story with many branches; the word 'theatre' is not always carved on them. It can therefore be difficult for the student of theatre, doing research at any level, to choose a topic and find the appropriate resources. The problem arises whether the project is for performance (for improvisation or play production), whether it is for written presentation (script or study) or whether it is simply reading. Suggestions are given below for research topics and projects related to each chapter. These have not been designed to be done exactly as written, but as a stimulus to teachers, students and general readers, to find their own topics and design their own projects. The scope of these should be carefully defined according to:

(1) the aim of the exercise – is it to be done in order to develop technical expertise, increased knowledge, critical appreciation or artistic creation?
(2) the participants – is it for individuals or for a group?
(3) the time, space and facilities available;
(4) the desired balance between specialisation and all-round development;
(5) the level of attainment already achieved by individuals or group – if a group, is it of mixed ability and experience?

It is hoped that these suggestions, modified according to the above limitations, will help to promote interesting and original work at secondary school or introductory college level. Where appropriate, plans, sketches, interviews and bibliography can be included.

2   The theatre event

(1) Choose a cultural community you are interested in researching. (It could be local or distant, native or foreign, historical or still existing.) Find out its chief festivals. Which of these are celebrated through drama? Study the origins, content, organisation and significance of such a theatre event.
(2) Choose a theatre or a theatre company and research its organisation, repertoire and general policy. (It could be local or distant, native or foreign, historical or still existing.) If it is an existing theatre or company, you may be able to interview people involved.
(3) Plan a theatre organisation or company in your neighbourhood, or in some other area that interests you. Devise the organisation, repertoire and general policy which would best suit the community.
(4) Create a festival of your own, in celebration of some event that is significant to your class or group.

3   Theatre space

(1) Compare and contrast the design and facilities of two or more theatre buildings. (Historical or modern, purpose-built or converted from other uses.) What factors influenced the design? How well does each serve its function in the community?
(2) Examine the work of a touring theatre company, assessing the problems they have – or had, if it is a past company – in adapting to different theatre spaces.
(3) Choose a space in your school, college or community to mount a production, outside or indoors. Assess the advantages and disadvantages of the space and suggest how any problems could be met. Alternatively, put this exercise into practice, mounting a production in a non-theatre space.
(4) Design a theatre, temporary or permanent, for a specific community.

(5) Produce a scene or play in two or more different spaces. Compare and contrast the effect.

4 Mask and costume

(1) Write a study on the use of masks, wigs, and/or make-up.
(2) Compare the use of costumes in everyday life and in the theatre.
(3) Explain how you would set about designing costumes for a play of your choice: either with a limited budget, or with an unlimited budget.
(4) Make a set of masks, costumes or puppets; use them to improvise a play.
(5) Examine the appearance of the clown or fool in theatre of different times and places.

5 The art of acting

(1) Study one or more methods of actor-training.
(2) Write a study of an individual actor, analysing his/her roles and methods. (The appropriate resource material includes pictures, criticism; films, tapes and videos of modern actors; interviews and live performances when accessible.)
(3) Study the portrayal of the same role by several different actors. (Same resource material as 2.)
(4) Study and practise one or more aspects of the art of acting: e.g. voice and speech; movement and mime; scene study; creating a role; make a final presentation.
(5) Examine the social role of the actor/actress in different communities.

6 The play

(1) Examine the role and status of the playwright in one or more cultures.
(2) Study and compare a selected group of plays:
    (a) by the same author, or
    (b) of the same period or place, or
    (c) dealing with similar ideas or characters, or
    (d) of the same genre, e.g. tragedy, comedy, one-character or two-character plays.

(3) Write your own play, by one of the following methods:
    (a) adapt an old play for a modern audience, or
    (b) choose a myth or story to dramatise, e.g. a modern version of Everyman, or
    (c) invent scenes of modern life that you would put in a time capsule to show future generations how people acted, what they thought and dreamed of in the twentieth century.

7   The scenic effect

(1) Study the work of an individual stage designer, or a group of designers, relating their work to specific productions and theatre spaces.

(2) Examine the scenic conventions used in one or more theatre traditions.

(3) Research the history of special effects in the theatre, e.g. fire, storms, snow, water and so on.

(4) Build a model stage and create scenery and lighting for it.

(5) Design the set for a specific play, using sketches, plans and descriptions. (Show clearly the size and shape of the theatre space you envisage.)

(6) Provide simple scenery and props for a production, arranging for it to be set, changed and struck (i.e. removed) where necessary.

(7) If you have sufficient experience, design and plot the lighting for a simple production.

8   Dance, music and sound

(1) Study one or more forms of dance-drama or musical theatre, such as: ritual and folk dances in primitive communities; dance-drama in India and/or South-East Asia; Italian opera; classical ballet; the American musical; modern ballet and dance.

(2) Study the use of music in plays by Shakespeare or Brecht, or some other plays where incidental music is significant.

(3) Examine the adaptation of a play into musical or dance form, e.g. *Othello* to Verdi's *Otello*, *Romeo and Juliet* to a ballet, or to Bernstein's *West Side Story*.

(4) Choose a myth or story and create a dance-drama based on it, using mime, solo dancers, dances for two or more, and ensemble dances. If you know how, transcribe it into choreographic notation.

(5) Improvise or compose scenes, or a play, in song. This may be comic or serious, with well-known tunes or original melodies. If you know how, transcribe and orchestrate.

(6) Explore some of these performance ideas:

    (a) Create a group ritual, in praise or in fear of something in the modern world, using words, chants, rhythm and movement.

    (b) Use everyday objects to assemble an 'orchestra'. Divide into two groups. One group creates the music, the other a dance in response to it. This can also be done in twos or in small groups.

    (c) Create a chorus, using words from a poem, story or newspaper, explored for their sound rather than their meaning.

9   The performance

(1) Study the work of one or more theatre critics.

(2) Compare reviews by several writers of one production, or of different productions of one play. (Bear in mind the readership of the reviews.)

(3) Write your own collection of theatre reviews perhaps with a specific reader or readership in mind.

(4) Compare the different kinds of audiences, (their type, behaviour and role) for theatre events in various times and places.

(5) If practicable conduct an audience survey, preparing a questionnaire and recording interviews with audience members. What conclusions can you draw from it? What recommendations could you make?

(6) Design a 'season' of theatre events for one of the following:

    (a) a repertoire for a theatre company;

    (b) a local festival of plays;

    (c) a package for a group of theatre visitors, selected from the plays showing in London or some other theatre centre.

10   The functions of theatre

(1) Study the work of one or more major theatre directors. What idea of theatre have they pursued? How have they put it into practice?

(2) Organise a debate on the following motion: The theatre contributes significantly to community life.

(3) Compare the number of people employed in two or more theatre companies. Could the various functions be fulfilled in other ways?

(4) Draw up a plan for a theatre of the future, explaining its purpose, organisation and programme.

(5) Examine the relationship between theatre and life.

Further study

THOSE seeking information about the theatre in the United States are faced with a wide array of opportunities for the pursuit of the needed data. Where only a casual interest in theatrical information is concerned, a visit to the local library and the use of such general reference works as encyclopedias or almanacs may satisfy the need. A greater interest in matters theatrical can be satisfied by referring to volumes in the library classed under Dewey numbers 792 and in the 800s and by referring to such indexes as *Readers' guide to periodical literature* and the *New York Times index*.

It is when faced with the need to research theatrical topics extensively that the major theatre collections in the United States come into play. Extensive collections of published works and archival materials relating to the theatre are the basis for the theatre collections of major university libraries in those universities which sponsor a drama school. Unlike public libraries, most university libraries classify their materials according to the Library of Congress classification scheme and under this arrangement works relating to the theatre are classed under the numbers PN2000–PN3299. Most academic libraries which are not state supported are private facilities and access to their collections must be approved. A major example of a university theatre collection would be that maintained by Yale University.

In addition to the university libraries there are several independent research libraries devoted to the field of theatre. The foremost independent theatre library in the United States is the Performing Arts Research Center of The New York Public Library. This library houses both a major archival and research collection and a circulating collection. Another important independent theatre library is that maintained by the Players Club in New York City.

The types of reference sources found in libraries and some important reference titles are listed below.

History

BROCKETT, OSCAR G. *History of the Theatre.* 5th ed. (Needham Heights, MA: Allyn & Bacon, 1987).

Editor's Note: These suggestions for further study were written by William B. Stern exclusively for the U.S. edition.

LONEY, GLENN. *20th Century Theatre* (New York: Facts on File, 1983). 2 volumes. A chronological record giving highlights of American premieres; British premieres; revivals and repertories; births, deaths, and debuts; theaters and productions from 1900 through 1979.

NAGLER, A.M. *Sources of Theatrical History* (New York: Theatre Annual, 1952). il. Lists sources from antiquity through the nineteenth century.

Biography

Who's Who in the Theatre. Ed 1–17 (London: Pitman, 1912–81). Irregular issues. Biographies of living actors, playwrights, directors, and others active in the London and New York theater.

Who's Who in the Theatre 1912–76. (Detroit: Gale, 1978). 4 volumes. A compilation of individuals dropped from *Who's Who in the Theatre* because of death or inactivity.

Contemporary Theatre, Film and Television. v. 1–   (Detroit: Gale, 1984). il. A revised and expanded continuation of *Who's Who in the Theatre.*

Indexes

The New York Times Directory of the Theatre. (New York: Arno Press, 1973). il. An index to theatre reviews presented in *The New York Times,* 1920–70. See **Reviews** for a compilation of the actual reviews.

Encyclopedias

Oxford Companion to the Theatre. 4th ed. (Oxford: Oxford University Press, 1983). An encyclopedic summary of theater throughout the world, with some emphasis on British and American theater. History and biography are major subjects.

BORDMAN, GERALD. *The American Musical Theatre; A Chronicle* (New York: Oxford University Press, 1986). Lists and describes all musicals known to have opened on Broadway through the 1984–85 season. Various biographical sketches and various indexes are included.

BORDMAN, GERALD. *Oxford Companion to American Theater* (New York: Oxford University Press, 1984). Somewhat similar to the *Oxford Companion to the Theatre* (listed above), but with the emphasis on the New York stage.

BRONNER, EDWIN. *Encyclopedia of the American Theatre 1900–1975.* (San Diego: A.S. Barnes, 1980). Gives extensive information about plays produced on or off Broadway during the period 1900–75.

Yearbooks

Best Plays. 1919–   (New York: Dodd Mead, 1919–   ). Condenses each of the ten best plays of the New York season and summarizes the theatrical season in New York and other cities.

Theatre World. 1944/45–   (New York: Theatre World, 1945–   ). il. Cast lists, dates, and several illustrations for each play produced on Broadway and many other American locations are printed here.

Reviews

The New York Times Theater Reviews 1870–   (New York: New York Times, 1971–   ). A number of volumes plus indexes; includes a chronological reprinting of reviews that appeared in *The New York Times.*

New York Theatre Critics' Review 1940–   (New York: New York Theatre Critics' Theatre Review 1940–   ). A yearly chronological reprinting of reviews as they originally appeared in all the major New York papers. Three indexes to these reviews are available.

Theatres

BOTTO, LOUIS. *At This Theatre* (New York: Dodd Mead & Co., 1984). An informal history of each Broadway theatre being served by *Playbill* magazine in 1984. A brief description of the theatre's opening and its leading attractions are presented.

Stubs (New York: M. Schattner, 1942–   ). Seating plan guide to Broadway theatres, plus some off-Broadway and others. New editions are issued irregularly.

Awards

The Tony Award (New York: Crown Publishing, 1984). Describes the Antoinette Perry (Tony) Award, probably considered the most prestigious of the various theatrical awards; lists, by season, the various nominees and winners from 1947 to 1984.

Periodicals

Theatre magazines with varying life spans—for example, *Theatre, Theatre Arts, The Stage*—have appeared throughout the twentieth century.

Index